W9-ALK-409

A GANNETT COMPANY

Lifeline

BIOGRAPHIES

NICKI MINAJ
Conquering Hip-Hop

by Felicity Britton

TFCB

Twenty-First Century Books · Minneapolis

Twenty-First Century Books
A division of Lerner Publishing Group, Inc.
241 First Avenue North
Minneapolis, MN 55401 U.S.A.

Website address: www.lernerbooks.com

Library of Congress Cataloging-in-Publication Data

Britton, Felicity.
    Nicki Minaj : conquering hip-hop / by Felicity Britton.
        p. cm. — (USA Today lifeline biographies)
    Includes bibliographical references and index.
    ISBN 978–1–4677–0810–4 (lib. bdg. : alk. paper)
    ISBN 978–1–4677–1060–2 (eBook)
    1. Minaj, Nicki—Juvenile literature. 2. Rap musicians—United States—Biography—
Juvenile literature. 3. Hip-hop—United States—Juvenile literature. I. Title.
ML3930.M64B75 2013
782.421649092—dc23 [B]   2012022905

Manufactured in the United States of America
1 – CG – 12/31/12

USA TODAY
A GANNETT COMPANY

Lifeline
BIOGRAPHIES

Ready to order? Before she made it big as an entertainer, Nicki Minaj worked in the restaurant business as a server.

From Mixtapes to Megastar

Onika Maraj was struggling. As a young woman, she was working all day in low-paying jobs and hustling her songs at night. After work, she would take the subway to meet with any music industry executives willing to hear her demo tapes. Nothing panned out. Her bosses didn't like her making calls about her music during work hours either. Eventually she was fired, just as she had been from her last ten jobs.

Onika decided to concentrate on her music full-time, even if she didn't make any money at it. She recorded and listened to her raps and beats over and over to improve her skills. She wrote for hours on end and recorded more songs. When she put some of her songs and photos up on Myspace.com, the head of Dirty Money Entertainment contacted her. His name was Fendi, and he produced a DVD magazine called *The Come Up*, featuring up-and-coming rappers. Fendi convinced Onika to change her name to Nicki Minaj and included her in several volumes, including *Volume 11*. This volume highlighted successful rapper Lil Wayne.

It was a phone call from Lil Wayne that would change Nicki Minaj's life forever. Nicki—the daughter of a nurse's aide and a crack addict father—would soon be the best-selling female rap artist in history. She would score two consecutive No. 1 albums, perform with Madonna at the Super Bowl Halftime Show, cause controversy at the Grammys, and sit in the front row at the hottest fashion shows in town.

Nicki is known as much for over-the-top outfits as she is for her outrageous rhymes and alter egos and for her business savvy. But she says this is just the beginning. Watch out Jay-Z, Diddy and other hip-hop moguls with multinational, multibrand empires—Nicki is determined to join your ranks!

Myspace: Nicki got her big break when a music executive discovered Nicki's music on her Myspace page in the early 2000s. The site is still a great place to learn more about Nicki's music, see photos and videos, and interact with Nicki and her friends.

Ocean view: Nicki's hometown is a suburb of Port of Spain, a city on the north-western coast of the island of Trinidad. The city looks out over the Gulf of Paria, which lies between Trinidad and the east coast of Venezuela in South America.

Dreams of Picket Fences

Nicki Minaj was born Onika Tanya Maraj on December 8, 1982 (some sources say 1984). She was born in Saint James, a suburb of Port of Spain, the capital of the Caribbean island nation of Trinidad and Tobago. Her mother, Carol, had five brothers and five sisters and many nieces and nephews. Onika was surrounded by aunts, uncles, and cousins. Onika's family called her Nicki. When she was three, her dad Robert (sometimes known as Omar) moved with Carol to the United States to look for work. "A lot of times, when you're from the islands, your parents leave and then send for you because it's easier when they have established themselves; when they have a place to stay, when they have a job" says Nicki. "I thought it was gonna be for a few days, it turned into two years without my mother."

Nicki and her older brother Jelani were left in the care of Carol's mother. Nicki recalls, "Growing up in Trinidad, I didn't know that we were poor, ten people living in a three-bedroom home and all the dogs and cats my grandmother had, none of that seemed really abnormal."

Nicki missed her parents terribly and looked forward to the day when they would all be reunited. She imagined that everyone in the United States was rich and lived in beautiful houses. She expected her parents would be living in a castle or at least have a white picket fence.

IN F⬤CUS

Trinidad and Tobago

The Republic of Trinidad and Tobago lies in the Caribbean Sea. The island nation is about the same size as the U.S. state of Delaware. Trinidad is the larger and more populated of the two main islands. Most of the nation's 1.3 million people live in Trinidad. The republic's capital is Port of Spain.

Trinidad and Tobago lie very close to the northeastern coast of Venezuela, South America. The climate is tropical, with a rainy season from June to December. Italian explorer Christopher Columbus sailed to Trinidad in 1498. The Spanish, for whom Columbus was working, ruled Trinidad until 1797. In that year, the British took over the island. British forces fought with the French and the Dutch over control of Tobago. That island changed hands twenty-two times before the British won control in 1803. The two islands became a single colony in 1888 and gained independence in 1962.

During the colonial years, Trinidad's main industry was growing sugar and cacao (cocoa beans). Workers on Tobago raised cotton and tobacco. In fact, the island's name may have come from the word *tobacco*. The people of Trinidad and Tobago are mainly of African or East Indian descent. Almost all speak English, the republic's official language. In the twenty-first century, the main industry is petroleum and related products (natural gas and petrochemicals).

Pop music: Growing up, Nicki loved the music of Whitney Houston *(above)*. She died in February 2012, and Nicki performed in memory of Houston at the 2012 Grammy Awards.

When her mother finally was able to bring Nicki and her brother to New York, Nicki was extremely disappointed. Not only was it cold and snowing there, but her new home was in a poor part of the New York City borough (district) of Queens. The house, on 147th Street off Rockaway Boulevard, had furniture in piles and was not luxurious at all.

Nicki's new neighborhood was South Jamaica, Queens, known as Southside. It is an area of one- and two-family houses, small apartment buildings, and large public housing projects. When Nicki and her family moved there, most residents were working-class African Americans and immigrants from Latin America and the Caribbean. Throughout Nicki's childhood, her mom constantly had music on in the house. Nicki loved the pop music of Whitney Houston, Cyndi Lauper, Madonna, and Enya.

IN FOCUS

South Jamaica, Queens

South Jamaica is a neighborhood in Queens, one of New York City's five boroughs. The neighborhood is also known as Southside and Southside Jamaica Queens. During the late 1800s, Irish immigrants settled in the area. In the 1950s, as white residents moved to the outer suburbs, middle-income African Americans moved into the area. In the late 1970s, Latin and West Indian immigrants settled there.

Many restaurants and stores in South Jamaica reflect South American and Caribbean cultures. Hair-braiding salons, Caribbean cuisine, soul food restaurants, and two malls cater to the needs of residents.

South Jamaica has produced many notable rappers. In addition to Nicki, Southside was home to 50 Cent, Lloyd Banks (also of G-unit), Waka Flocka Flame, Ja Rule, and many others.

Walking the avenue: Jamaica Avenue is the main street in the South Jamaica neighborhood in Queens, New York, where Nicki's family settled after they came to the United States.

Tough start: Curtis James Jackson III (50 Cent) was born in South Jamaica. He has since created a highly successful career for himself as a recording artist, record producer, actor, and businessman.

Later, Nicki got into rap, including Lauryn Hill, Missy Elliott, and her fellow Southsider 50 Cent. She also loved fashion and remembers her first American coat. Made from pink corduroy with brown buttons and fur on the inside of the hood, it was her first piece of winter clothing. She adored it.

Fear and Loathing

In the 1980s, many people in Southside suffered from addiction to crack cocaine. Highly organized drug crews made huge profits selling to crack addicts there. Drug dealers were violent and murdered anyone who didn't pay or who tried to sell crack in areas they considered their territory.

Carol worked as a nurse's aide, and Robert worked for the credit card company American Express. When Robert lost his job, he slid into alcohol and crack addiction. To pay for drugs, Nicki's father would sell the family's furniture and other personal possessions. When drinking, his moods would often turn violent. Nicki remembers her parents arguing and screaming. In fits of rage, her father punched holes in the walls. Because of her father's violence, the police were often called to her home. Nicki and her brother feared their father. Nicki often ran to

IN F⊙CUS

The Crack Epidemic

Cocaine is an illegal stimulant made from the leaves of the coca plant. It is usually sold in powder form. In the 1980s, an oversupply of cocaine led to a dramatic drop in the drug's price. Drug dealers were losing money. So they decided to convert the powder to "crack," a smokable form of cocaine. It was easy to produce. And it was inexpensive to buy. One dose cost as little as $2.50.

Crack is highly addictive. At first, most crack users were white and middle class. But because crack was so inexpensive, it became popular in a wide range of communities. By the mid-1980s, crack addiction had become a serious problem around the country. Cocaine-related hospital emergencies increased 400 percent. The crack trade led to violence, and crack-related murders in many large cities skyrocketed. In addition, pregnant women who were addicted to crack exposed their babies to the drug. When these "crack babies" were born, they often had birth defects, attention deficit disorder, and various developmental problems.

Busted: Crack cocaine (*above*) is the most addictive form of the illegal drug cocaine.

the neighbor's house for safety. She even had nightmares that Robert would kill her mom. Her worries about her mother's safety were not exaggerated.

One night, Nicki claims Robert tried to burn the house down while her mother was inside. The previous night, Carol had dreamed that the house was burning. She sent Nicki and Jelani to a friend's house to sleep the next night. That night the screeching of sirens woke them up. They ran the five blocks to their home, which was going up in flames. Carol barely escaped alive. Nicki detailed the experience in a song called "Autobiography."

Nicki was bitterly disappointed in her father. When she said her prayers, she knelt at the edge of the bed praying that one day she would be rich enough to take care of her mother. Nicki believed that if she could become a famous soap opera star like the ones her mother and grandmother loved, she would have enough money to take Carol and Jelani to safety, far from their father. The three of them moved several times to try to flee Robert. But Nicki says her dad always found them. The violence only stopped when Jelani became old enough and big enough to stand up to Robert. Although Nicki's mom backs up Nicki's story, Robert claims Nicki's version of events is exaggerated.

Throughout Nicki's childhood, Carol took Nicki and her brother to church. She hoped they would find encouragement in the words and stories of the Bible. She wanted them to have the courage to get through the tough times. Nicki also found ways to escape the trauma of her home life through reading books. She loved stories about normal families with lovely houses and nice things. She created a rich fantasy life for herself too. She invented funny accents and pretended to be a teacher, a nurse, and other characters.

Nicki went to several different elementary schools as her family bounced from house to house. At Public School (P.S.) 45, Nicki's fifth-grade teacher was Elizabeth Smith-Breslin. Nicki never admitted to her that there was trouble at home. But Smith-Breslin could sense it.

November 23, 2010

Nicki Minaj Brings Her Theatrical Style to *Pink Friday* [Excerpt 1]

From the Pages of
USA TODAY

For all her flamboyant self-assurance, Nicki Minaj admits that her creative expression is rooted in a desire for "emotional escape," stemming from a troubled childhood. She was born Onika Maraj in Trinidad, where she spent her first years living with her maternal grandmother while her parents forged a life as immigrants in Queens, N.Y.

Minaj arrived in Queens around age 4, expecting to find "a wealthy family, because when you're little and you're from a different country, you think all Americans are rich." Instead, she discovered that her mother, then a nurse's aide, was struggling to make ends meet, while her father fought his own battle with drugs and alcohol.

As a child, Minaj remembers "kneeling at the foot of my mother's bed every morning, saying, 'Please, God, make me rich and famous so that I can take care of her.' She would watch soap operas, and so would my grandmother in Trinidad, so that was the connection I made: I could become a soap opera star and make a lot of money, and my mother and brother and me could sneak away and my father would never find us."

Minaj did study drama, as a teenager at New York's LaGuardia High School. After graduating, she juggled odd jobs before deciding to focus on music. "I wrote, made underground mixtapes, sold CDs out of my car." Her luck changed when a DVD featuring her songs fell into [Lil] Wayne's hands. "I was still so wet behind the ears. I didn't think hip-hop would embrace my theatrical side; I was nervous about that. But I feel like over the past year fans and the media have allowed me to be who I am."

She also made peace with her parents, though her relationship with her dad "is still strained." The couple [her parents] now has a third child, a 12-year-old boy, and Minaj bought them a new home.

—Elysa Gardner

Hooked on drama: The Fiorello H. LaGuardia High School of Music & Art and Performing Arts, where Nicki went to high school, is named after Fiorello La-Guardia. He was mayor of New York from 1934 until 1945.

She took Nicki under her wing, encouraging her creativity. She was amused by Nicki's dramatic flair and accents and cast her in the class play. Her support was life-changing for Nicki, who began to believe she could really be an entertainer.

Performing Arts

Starting in sixth grade, Nicki attended Elizabeth Blackwell Middle School 210, home to more than two thousand students. She joined the band there and learned to play the clarinet. Inspired by an older neighbor, Nicki started writing rhymes and rapping when she was about eleven. She wrote about simple, easy topics—such as cookies—that reflected her young age. Older kids paid attention to her songs and encouraged her to stick with it.

When it was time to pick a high school, Nicki and her mom headed to Manhattan (one of New York's five boroughs). Nicki wanted to study the performing arts. So she auditioned at Manhattan's Fiorello H. LaGuardia High School of Music & Art and Performing Arts. The school is famous. It was the setting for the movie *Fame* (1980, 2009) and the TV series (1982–1987) of the same name. Students at the school are looking for professional careers in dance, drama, the visual arts, and vocal and instrumental music. Famous alumni (former students) of LaGuardia include actors Jennifer Aniston and Robert De Niro and singers Liza Minnelli, Slick Rick, and Azealia Banks. Nicki first auditioned for singing. However, she had hurt her voice that day and was quite hoarse. Nicki did poorly at her audition and wasn't accepted. She was devastated.

Carol suggested that she should try out for drama. Nicki didn't want to. But her mother insisted that she give it a try. Frustrated with her mother, Nicki stomped down to the school's basement, where the drama auditions were being held. She watched other students perform. Within twenty minutes, she was hooked. She felt completely at home because the other students were as dramatic and theatrical as she was. This time, her audition went well and the school accepted her as a drama major. Looking back, she's very glad she listened to her mother!

Loves Drama

Nicki found that LaGuardia had an exciting mix of singers, dancers, actors, and artists. She was surprised to find that she wasn't the only kid in the world who put on fake accents and was totally dramatic. Students at LaGuardia worked hard to stand out and get noticed. They sang and danced in the hallway, and everyone had an individual fashion sense. They remember her as funny, talented, and confident. Nicki was one of only three black kids in her class. Although she was at school to learn acting, she continued to sing and rap in her spare time.

While she was at LaGuardia, Nicki made an impulsive decision. When she was sixteen, she got a tattoo on her left arm. She chose a series of Chinese characters that mean "God is always with me." Nicki says she completely regrets getting the tattoo. She feels

Translation: The tattoo on Nicki's arm means "God is always with me."

embarrassed about how it looks when she's wearing a ball gown or other formal wear. She believes sixteen is too young to get a tattoo. She advises teens to wait until they are at least twenty-one years old. By then, people have a better sense of what they want in life and whether a tattoo is a smart decision. Around the same time, Nicki got her tongue pierced. Her mother hated it and the tattoo. Nicki got rid of the tongue ring but was stuck with the tattoo.

Each year, LaGuardia hosts a performance showcase of seniors for talent agents and managers. If they see a performer they like, they give that person a special slip. In Nicki's senior year, several agents gave her slips. She was ecstatic! Nicki thought these agents would send

USA TODAY Snapshots®

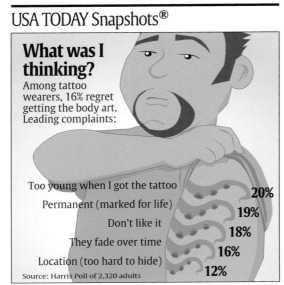

What was I thinking?
Among tattoo wearers, 16% regret getting the body art. Leading complaints:

Too young when I got the tattoo — 20%
Permanent (marked for life) — 19%
Don't like it — 18%
They fade over time — 16%
Location (too hard to hide) — 12%

Source: Harris Poll of 2,320 adults

By Michelle Healy and Veronica Salazar, USA TODAY, 2008

her on auditions and find acting jobs for her. However, she was soon disillusioned. She had no luck reaching the agents by phone to set up meetings. And Nicki desperately wanted to earn her own money. She wanted to pay for a place of her own and to buy a car. She especially wanted a white BMW. So to make money, she started waitressing at restaurants such as Red Lobster. She earned twelve dollars an hour plus tips.

Customer service was not a strong point for the sassy, opinionated Nicki, however. For this reason, she was fired from many jobs. Once a manager yelled at Nicki for dropping one of her acrylic nails in a customer's salad. Nicki agreed with the manager's concern but for a different reason. That fingernail was expensive! Red Lobster fired her for chasing a customer into the parking lot. She had walked out of the restaurant with Nicki's pen, which she had used to sign the credit card slip. In the parking lot, Nicki tapped on her car window and gave her the finger.

While working full-time, Nicki was finally able to arrange for some auditions on her own. In 2001 she landed a role in an off-Broadway play called *In Case You Forget*. The play is about a graffiti artist about to be sent to jail for vandalism. For rehearsals, she would show up straight from work in her waitress uniform. Her cast mates teased her for not bringing them food from the restaurant where she was working. Nicki soon lost patience with acting, though. She felt her career wasn't moving forward fast enough. So she decided to focus on her music instead. Nicki juggled her nine-to-five restaurant job with after-hours writing, recording, and meetings with music executives.

All Work and No Play

Nicki had an exhausting schedule. She worked her regular job all day and then worked on her music all night. She would take the subway all over New York to meet with anyone who might listen to her demo or who might have music industry contacts. But she felt as if she wasn't having any success. People were always slamming doors in her face. She was depressed and knew she wouldn't be able to keep up the pace for much longer. When she was fired once again from a day job, Nicki made a decision. She would concentrate full-time on her music and give it her all. Her mom was worried about Nicki's decision. She encouraged her to go to college instead, but Nicki was determined. She knew she couldn't expect to be successful by working on her music only part-time.

Focusing full-time on her music, Nicki worked every day for hours on her rhymes and beats. Finally, one of her meetings paid off when a

IN F**O**CUS

Safaree

Safaree Lloyd Samuels was born on June 3, 1981. His nicknames include SB, Scaff Beezy, VVS Beezy, and Scaff Breezy. Safaree was a member of the group Hood$tars, cowriting songs and rapping. Nicki has known him for a long time. She trusts him and is rarely seen without him. His official title is Nicki Minaj's Hype Man. He is also her best friend, assistant, nerve soother, and trusted adviser. Safaree is often rumored to be Nicki's boyfriend and fiancé. Publicly, she says he's more like a brother. Nicki credits him with finding great beats for her, and she listed him as coexecutive producer on her album *Roman Reloaded* (2012).

Hype man: Nicki has known Safaree "SB" Samuels (*left*) since early in her career. The two are very close, and the media loves to gossip about the nature of their relationship.

production company agreed to give her free studio time to record some sample tracks. Nicki worked tirelessly, constantly writing, rewriting, and then recording. She says her faith in God, plus a fear of what would happen to her family if she couldn't bring in money, was what got her through the hardest days. In 2002 a New York rap group called the Hood$tars asked Nicki to join them. Safaree "SB" Samuels was a member of the group.

Talent spotter: Bowlegged Lou *(above, in 2005)* believed in Nicki's talent early on, when the rap world had few female stars.

Another member of the Hood$tars was Lou$tar, the son of Full Force's Bowlegged Lou (Lucien George Jr.). Full Force had produced work for performing artists such as Britney Spears, Rihanna, James Brown, Backstreet Boys, Lil' Kim, and Lisa Lisa. Bowlegged Lou thought Nicki had potential as a solo star. He took her under his wing.

For the next three years, Bowlegged Lou tried to get Nicki signed to a record label. It was during this time that Nicki recorded the song "Autobiography," a revealing number about her traumatic childhood. Bowlegged Lou and Nicki visited labels including Def Jam/Roc-A-Fella and G-Unit, but at that time, no label or rap crew wanted a female rapper. Nicki parted ways with Bowlegged Lou and struck out on her own again. She uploaded her songs to Myspace and started gaining fans. When she performed in small clubs in New York, Nicki was thrilled to note that everyone in the audience already knew the words of her songs from her Myspace page.

May 20, 2011

Attention students: Nicki Minaj is 'principal for the day'

<u>From the Pages of</u>
<u>USA TODAY</u>

Keeping kids in schools these days is a challenge, with a whopping 1.2 million students dropping out of school every year, according to the White House.

But incentives can change everything. Just ask non-profit Get Schooled, which launched its own challenge this spring—the Get MotivatED Challenge—a six-week competition among 25 high schools nationwide to improve daily attendance with some pretty sweet prizes at stake. Not only did the Collins Academy High School in Chicago [Illinois]—the winner—receive three $10,000 college scholarships for its top students, the school also received a surprise visit from a major superstar *and* high school grad on Thursday.

Acting as 'principal for the day', singer Nicki Minaj showed up to congratulate the 400 students and teachers at the Collins Academy for their hard work in maintaining a 92% attendance rate throughout the challenge, an important feat as studies show that the rate of attendance is one of the most significant predictors of dropping out. A graduate of LaGuardia High School in New York City, Minaj had an important message to share with the kids—that education has been key to her success.

"I am a young, female mogul before I am an artist. As a businesswoman there

Wayne's World

The photos on Nicki's Myspace site caught the attention of record label executive Fendi. As the CEO of Dirty Money Records, he released hip-hop DVDs. Fendi recalls, "Back then, when you landed on someone's page the music would start playing. I'm on her page and the music starts playing and I'm like 'who is this? This can't be shorty [a woman].

Rethink P[...]

Present: Nicki *(front row center)* visited the students at Collins Academy High School in Chicago in May 2011. She was there to congratulate them for their high attendance rate.

isn't a single day where I don't use my education or acquire new knowledge to ensure my success. Regardless of where you are today, with education you can take yourself where you want to be," she says.

In addition to the $30,000 scholarships to the three Collins Academy students, 12 students at four other competing schools in Boston, Philadelphia, Nashville and Chicago are each receiving $1,000 scholarships from Comcast as a reward for their impressive efforts.

To learn more about the Get MotivatED Challenge, visit https://getschooled.com.

—Christie Garton

This [music] sounds hard.'" Fendi contacted Nicki and signed her to Dirty Money. He also convinced her to change her last name to Minaj. Nicki didn't like the new name, but Fendi says, "I fought with her and as you can see I won the argument."

Fendi worked to increase Nicki's fan base. For example, he produced a popular DVD magazine called *The Come Up*. This digital magazine features videotaped interviews and music from hot, under-ground rappers. Fendi included Nicki's raps on several of the DVDs, and fans loved it.

One of Nicki's dreams had always been to meet Lil Wayne, the super successful MC (a hip-hop term for "master of ceremonies" and for "microphone controller"). Wayne had top-selling albums such as *Tha Carter* and *Tha Carter II*. *Tha Carter II* had debuted at No. 2 on the *Billboard* 200 Album chart in 2005, selling more than two million cop-ies. So in *Volume 11* (called "The Carter Edition") of *The Come Up*, Fendi placed footage of Nicki freestyling (improvising her rapping) after the interview with Lil Wayne. Fendi says, "I knew Wayne was gonna watch it. I knew as soon as he watched the DVD he was gonna give me a call. Wayne hit me and was like 'I wanna sign this chick Nicki. Who is she?' I was doing a party with Lil Wayne in Greensboro [North Carolina] and I flew Nicki out to meet him and the rest is history."

Up and running: Lil Wayne (*left*) helped Nicki (*center*) release her first CDs. Here, she appears with Wayne and Mack Maine (*right*) of Young Money Entertainment on Black Entertainment Television's *The Mo'Nique Show* in 2009.

Young Money

Nicki was excited about meeting Lil Wayne. He had been one of her idols for many years. Born Dwayne Michael Carter Jr., Wayne started rapping when he was eight years old. Cash Money Records signed him to their label when he was only nine years old. They were impressed with the freestyle raps he kept leaving on the answering machine of the label's owner.

Wayne dropped out of high school when he was fourteen years old to pursue a hip-hop career. He never dreamed that one day he would be president of Cash Money, guiding young rappers and running his own label. But by the time he was in his twenties, he was a seasoned veteran of the music scene. At the age of twenty-five, he became president of Cash Money. He was free to sign new artists to Cash Money or to his own imprint, Young Money Entertainment. When Wayne saw Nicki's freestyle on *The Come Up*, his response was instant. "I was like, this female right here is amazing. She'd be amazing for my label as well, and so that's when I knew I wanted to sign her, as soon as I heard her, as soon as I saw her. Get me in contact with that . . . girl named Nicki!"

Playtime Is Over

In Greensboro, North Carolina, Nicki and Wayne discussed her goals and planned the next steps. He felt the secret was to create buzz about Nicki on the streets, to give her street credibility. Nicki moved to Atlanta, Georgia, which had a thriving rap scene. With Wayne's help, she signed up to perform at clubs three to four times a week. Wayne helped her release a number of mixtapes. These "underground" CDs are not distributed by major record labels. They are designed to get unknown artists some exposure before they hit the mainstream. Nicki's mixtapes included *Playtime Is Over* (2007) and *Sucka Free* (2008).

Nicki came out hard. She gave her all, wanting to prove she was a good rapper. Her lyrics were often sexually explicit and full of cursing, just like those of male MCs. Nicki chose this style on purpose. She wanted to make her way in the male-dominated world of hip-hop. "I always wanted to play with the boys," she says. "I didn't want to be a pawn in their game or have a sidekick role. I wanted to be more of a lead character—a superhero." The mixtapes sold well. They showcased her talent and swagger, and many listeners soon became fans.

Nicki was chomping at the bit to release an album. Wayne felt it was important to build Nicki's reputation and credibility slowly. He didn't want to launch her on the scene so fast that listeners would feel she was a manufactured talent. The Nicki Minaj on the mixtapes was raw, uncensored, and tough. On these tapes, she had a chance to experiment with different rhythms, intonations, and voices. She showed off her unique combinations of eccentric and cartoonish, brash and bossy, sweet and naive, powerful and aggressive. She could move between the sound of an innocent girl to that of a street-smart know-it-all. She also showed a talent for clever wordplay and frantic delivery.

In addition, Nicki loved to sing as well as rap on her tapes. This mix of singing and rapping is unusual in hip-hop, where performers tend only to rap. All of this helped Nicki develop a strong sense of who she wanted to be as a performer.

In June 2008, Lil Wayne released his album *Tha Carter III*. It reached No. 1 on the U.S. and Canadian charts. The album sold more than three and a half million copies and was followed by the I Am Music Tour (December 2008–April 2009). Combined with the Young Money Presents: America's Most Wanted Music Festival (a series of concerts featuring Young Money artists), the tour brought in more than $42

Family: Members of the Young Money family, who mentored Nicki early on, perform at a music video shoot for Lil Wayne's song "Every Girl" in 2009. Pictured are *(from left)* Lil Chuckee, Lil Twist, Lil Wayne, Gudda Gudda, and Drake.

million, breaking hip-hop tour records. Lil Wayne showcased Nicki during this tour, exposing her to huge audiences.

Nicki took advantage of her new celebrity, making contacts and requesting guest features for her next mixtape, *Beam Me Up Scotty* (2009). The CD featured fellow Young Money artists Drake, Gudda Gudda, Shanell, and Lil Wayne. It also had guest spots from Gucci Mane, Ricky Blaze, Busta Rhymes, and Bobby Valentino. Having that many high-quality features was unheard of for an unsigned artist. The mixtape showed off Nicki's rapid rapping style and clever rhymes and was chosen by MTV's *Mixtape Daily* as its weekly pick on May 4, 2009. Critics praised her entertaining lyrics and great flow. The song "I Go Crazy" (featuring Lil Wayne) even gained airplay on radio and made it to No. 20 on the *Billboard* Hot Rap Songs chart.

Through the tour and her mixtapes, Nicki gained thousands of new fans. She also spent a lot of time on Twitter and Myspace developing a relationship with her followers. By the summer of 2009, big record labels were aware of Nicki's talent and wanted to sign her. For example, in August, Warner Brothers made an offer that Nicki chose to turn down. Instead, she officially signed to Young Money.

Guest Star

In December 2009, Nicki was ecstatic to get a call from singer Mariah Carey's team. Mariah was remixing a song from *Memoirs of an Imperfect Angel*, her twelfth studio album. The remix (a version that mixes and rerecords elements of an original song) was to include a guest vocal. Mariah wanted Nicki to be the featured artist. As a little girl, Nicki idolized Mariah and sang Mariah's songs in front of the mirror. She couldn't believe she was actually going to share a song with her! Often singers record their vocals separately and they are later mixed together in the studio. But Mariah invited Nicki to record the song "Up Out My Face" together. Nicki says she imagined Mariah would be distant and aloof. After all, Mariah was planning another album. Nicki hadn't even had a first studio release.

But Mariah was funny and silly and totally down to earth. The pair made a video, directed by Mariah's husband, Nick Cannon. In it, Nick and Mariah burst out of doll boxes playing life-sized dolls, nurses, and friends on a spa date. The song was designed to be the lead single for Mariah's upcoming album *Angels Advocate*. Soon after the release of "Up Out My Face," the album was canceled. Promotion of the track was canceled too. All the same, it reached No. 39 on the *Billboard* Hot R & B/Hip-Hop Songs chart.

That same month, Wayne released *We Are Young Money*. This studio album showcased all the Young Money artists. The talent on the album included Drake, Tyga, Lil Twist, Lil Chuckee, T-Streets, Short Dawg, Shanell, Jae Millz, Gudda Gudda, Mack Maine, Birdman, Lloyd, Gucci Mane—and Nicki. Nicki collaborated on five songs. The album was immediately popular, debuting at No. 9 on the *Billboard* 200 chart. One of the standout tracks was "Bedrock," performed by Lil Wayne, Drake, Tyga, Gudda Gudda, Jae Millz, Nicki, and featuring R & B singer Lloyd. "Bedrock" hit No. 2 on the US *Billboard* Hot 100 chart and No. 9 on the Singles Chart in the United Kingdom. Suddenly everyone wanted to know about this female rapper, Nicki Minaj.

Nicki's cameo on "Bedrock" almost didn't happen, though. She remembers working in the studio with Wayne in New Orleans, Louisiana, listening to the other guest spots and feeling that the song was going to be a big hit. She had written some verses and really wanted to be featured on the song. But that afternoon, she had to fly out to do a show in Atlanta. When she returned the next morning, she went directly from the airport to the studio. Wayne was angry with her. He questioned her work ethic because she had chosen her club concert over his song. He told her she'd been taken off the record. Nicki was crushed. To prove her commitment to the album, she worked really hard on some new verses. She headed to Wayne's house to show him her work. He let her spit some rhymes, and when she saw him smile, she was flooded with relief. Yes! She was back on the song.

"Bedrock" was a huge success. Other recording artists were

Guest stars: Rapper Yo Gotti *(right)* and Nicki perform on a Black Entertainment Television (BET) New Year's Eve special in 2009. Gotti was one of many artists who invited Nicki to record with him early in her career.

impressed with Nicki and wanted her to guest on their records. She recorded the song "5 Star Chick" with Yo Gotti. Over time she graduated to singing with bigger and bigger music industry names such as Usher, Christina Aguilera, Robin Thicke, and Rihanna. Even in this celebrity company, Nicki held her own and often stole the show on the records.

In January 2010, Young Money released another unofficial mixtape. It was mostly a collection of other people's songs on which Nicki had been featured. The mixtape did include a few previously unreleased songs such as "Your Love." The song sampled the melody of pop star Annie Lennox's cover of the ballad "No More 'I Love You's'" (1995). In previous songs, Nicki had referred to herself as Nicki the Ninja, Nicki Lewensky, Nicki Da Boss, and Harajuku Barbie. This mixtape put the Barbie persona in the forefront. It was called *Barbie World* and featured a cover image of Nicki in the familiar Barbie box.

On Twitter, Nicki started signing off on some of her posts as "It's

USA TODAY

Life

SECTION D

LIFE.USATODAY.COM

December 2, 2010

Billboard ranks celebs' social status on the Web

From the Pages of
USA TODAY

Next time you become of a fan of a favorite musician on Facebook, you may be helping them inch their way up a chart. *Billboard*'s new Social 50 recognizes the online popularity of celebs on social networking sites, with Rihanna coming out on top of the chart's debut week.

To come up with the rankings, a formula takes into account weekly additions of friends/fans/followers along with weekly artist page views and weekly song plays on MySpace, YouTube, Facebook, Twitter and iLike—but friends'/fans' behavior takes precedence, followed by artist page views and song plays. The final ranking also includes a unique metric measuring the ratio of page views to fans. Rounding out the top five this week is Justin Bieber, Eminem, Lady Gaga and Nicki Minaj. The chart will appear on Billboard.com and Billboard.biz every Thursday, and in *Billboard* magazine every week.

—Cindy Clark

Barbie, b—ch." Her followers began referring to her as Barbie, and she nicknamed her female fans Barbies, or Barbz for short. She called her male fans Ken dolls, or Kens.

In April 2010, Nicki released the single "Massive Attack" featuring rapper Sean Garrett. The song was originally planned as part of what was to be her debut album. Cash Money (the parent company of Young Money) paid for a $500,000 video to support the song. In the video, Nicki and Sean perform in jungle and desert scenes. Nicki wears

a range of sexy, brightly col-
ored outfits and wigs. In
a repeating cut, Nicki and
model-actress Amber Rose
drive through the desert
in a hot pink Lamborghini,
chased by a military heli-
copter. But even with the
glitzy video, the song failed
to make an impact and was
dropped from the upcoming
album.

Breaking Records

In June 2010, Nicki reluc-
tantly released an official
version of the song "Your
Love." An inferior version
had been leaked online
without the permission of
Nicki or her label. Radio sta-

Costar: Sean Garrett appeared with Nicki
in her *Massive Attack* video. Originally
from Atlanta, Georgia, Garrett is a singer-
songwriter, a rapper, and a very successful
record producer.

tions picked up the song and played it on the air. Nicki was distraught
by the poor quality of the recording. She says, "I . . . was really upset.
[The track they were using] wasn't mixed, it wasn't finished, it wasn't
anything—I wasn't gonna use it at all. But then radio started playing
it." But the tune was a hit. So Nicki quickly recorded additional lyrics,
mixed it, and released it as the second single for her upcoming album.

The song went to No. 1 on *Billboard*'s Hot Rap Songs chart. With
this ranking, Nicki became the first female rapper in eight years to
have a No. 1 hit. (Lil' Kim had seen the No. 1 spot in a cameo on 50
Cent's "Magic Stick" seven years earlier. But Missy Elliot and her song
"Work It" from 2002 was the most recent recording to take the No. 1
position for best solo female rapper.)

Center stage: Nicki performed with Jay-Z *(left)* and Kanye West *(right)* in New York's Yankee Stadium in September 2010. Kanye praised Nicki's amazing talent and predicted she would go far in the world of rap.

Nicki followed up with the song "Right Thru Me" in September. The recording mixed Nicki's singing with her signature animated, fast raps. Along the way, she found time to write more verses and to be featured on tracks with Ludacris, Trey Songz, and other artists. By October Nicki had made history by having the most singles on *Billboard*'s Hot 100 chart at one time.

Respect from Peers

Later that month, hip-hop mega star Kanye West released his controversial track "Monster." The song features verses by fellow hip-hop giant Jay-Z, rapper Rick Ross, folksinger Bon Iver, and Nicki. Listeners widely agreed that Nicki outshone Jay-Z and Kanye. Kanye told Angie Martinez on Hot 97, a popular radio station for hip-hop and rap music, "The scariest artist in the game right now . . . the scariest artist is definitely Nicki Minaj. And I think she has the most potential out of everyone to be the No. 2 rapper of all time 'cause nobody's gonna be

October 10, 2010

Nicki Minaj wins big at BET Hip-Hop Awards

From the Pages of
USA TODAY

Nicki Minaj was a big winner Saturday at the 2010 BET Hip-Hop Awards in Atlanta. She took home three trophies—Rookie of the Year, People's Champ and the Made-You-Look award, a nod to her fashion flair. "I'm paving the way for girls," she said, according to HipandPop.com. "I wanna thank all the girls of hip-hop."

—Ann Oldenburg /Lifeline Live

BET trophy: Nicki accepts her award for Rookie of the Year at the 2010 BET Hip-Hop Awards in Atlanta, Georgia. The BET Awards were established in 2001 to recognize African Americans and other minorities in the entertainment world.

bigger than Eminem. Eminem's the No. 1 rapper of all time."

Rapper Rick Ross also became a believer. "[Seeing her work on "Monster"] was the day Nicki Minaj earned my respect as a lyricist," he says. "Before that day she was a great entertainer, but for me to get in the studio with my own two eyes and see her write her verse, I knew that was gonna be one of the greatest verses of this year."

The song was hailed as the best collaboration of the year. Nicki beat out all her male counterparts to win best verse of the year from the hip-hop website HipHopDX. The verse contrasted Nicki's brash aggression with her sweet, innocent act. Nicki had reached a point in her career where she was earning the sort of money for writing verses that was normally paid to proven industry veterans. And she hadn't even released an album yet.

NICKI MINAJ *Pink* FRID

Pretty in pink: The cover of Nicki's first album, *Pink Friday*, features Nicki as her Barbie persona. The character is a fun, sexy, imaginative young woman who likes all things pink.

Pink Friday Lands

▪▪▪▪

Anticipation was building for Nicki's first studio release, due to come out in November 2010. Fans had loved her guest spots, but they were only bite-sized pieces. Listeners wanted to see if Nicki could deliver on a full-length album of solo performances. Titled *Pink Friday*, the album was available for preordering on Amazon in October. Six weeks before it was released, *Pink*

Friday was already No. 4 on the Amazon charts. When *Pink Friday* dropped on November 19, 2010, it debuted at No. 2 on the *Billboard* 200 chart. Combining rap, R & B, and a splash of pop, the album had broad appeal. It sold 375,000 copies in the first week.

On December 7, 2010, a third single from the album was released. "Moment 4 Life" featured Young Money artist Drake. The video is a play on the familiar Cinderella story. In the video's introduction, Nicki plays two roles—herself, in a long blue dress, and a fairy godmother, all in pink. Nicki's character goes to a ball, where she meets a handsome man played by Drake. The two marry and share a kiss as the clock strikes midnight. For fans in the know, this was a humorous take on rumors that Nicki and Drake were romantically involved in real life. And, in fact, both Nicki and Drake had tweeted about the two getting married. The couple wasn't actually engaged. But the buzz helped the song peak at No. 13 on the *Billboard* Hot 100. It became Nicki's first solo U.K. Top 40 hit.

"Moment 4 Life" showed off Nicki's flair for dramatic acting. It also introduced some of her invented characters, such as Martha, the fairy godmother. Martha is the mother of another character Nicki created— Roman Zolanski. When acting as Roman, Nicki is crass, spiteful, and theatrical. In

Creating buzz: Nicki and rapper-actor Drake *(right)* used social networking to fuel romantic rumors about the two performers.

USA TODAY
Life
SECTION D
LIFE.USATODAY.COM

November 23, 2011

Billboard honoring
Nicki Minaj as rising star

From the Pages of USA TODAY

Nicki Minaj will have another moment to savor from her super year: *Billboard* is honoring her as its rising star of 2011.

She is slated to get the honor at *Billboard*'s Women in Music event on Dec. 2 in New York City.

Minaj said Wednesday she was "deeply honored to be recognized by *Billboard*." She said she and her fans have come a "mighty long way" but are not close to where "God will take us."

The rapper and singer has emerged as one of music's most popular entertainers since releasing her debut album *Pink Friday* late last year. Her hits include "Super Bass" and "Moment 4 Life." She'll have one of her biggest fans on hand as well: Taylor Swift is also being honored as the woman of the year.

—Associated Press

---

contrast, Martha is very prim and proper and speaks with a British accent. In other videos, Nicki had introduced a wide-eyed character nicknamed Barbie (after the Mattel doll). Nicki has said that the different characters represent different parts of her personality, so they are often called her alter egos. As an actor, playing different roles is fun for Nicki.

In January 2011, Nicki achieved yet another dream. She was chosen as the musical act for *Saturday Night Live*. As a native New Yorker, Nicki was thrilled to have the chance to be on the iconic late-night comedy

Live from New York: Nicki performed two songs on the January 29, 2011, episode of late-night television's *Saturday Night Live*. She dressed as Martha, the mother of Roman Zolanski, another of Nicki's characters.

show. She performed two songs on the show—"Moment 4 Life" and "Right Thru Me"—and joined the cast for two skits. For the skit called "The Creep," she joined Andy Samberg and filmmaker John Waters. Nicki's character wore thick black glasses and a nerdy too-small suit and tie. She and her costars instructed viewers how to properly do a move called the Creep. In the second skit, "Bride of Blackenstein," Nicki played a sassy-mouthed, curvaceous mate for Blackenstein (a Frankenstein-like monster). Nicki recorded the show on DVR at home so she could watch it afterward, just to convince herself that it had really happened.

Meanwhile, sales of *Pink Friday* continued to climb. On January 5, 2011, the album was certified platinum by the Recording Industry Association of America (RIAA). In February it reached the No. 1 position on the *Billboard* charts. "Super Bass," a bonus track from the deluxe edition of *Pink Friday*, was both a critical and chart success.

USA TODAY

Life

SECTION D

LIFE.USATODAY.COM

November 22, 2010

Listen Up: Thank God for Nicki Minaj's *Pink Friday*

<u>From the Pages of</u>
<u>USA TODAY</u>

Nicki Manaj's *Pink Friday* swerves effortlessly from hard-core rap to sweet pop bliss.

The female rapper mixes Barbie-doll cute and hard-core grit into a frothy concoction that's guaranteed to have wide appeal.

Hip-hop has always been a testosterone-fueled genre that has had little room for female MCs.

Enter Nicki Minaj—a talented rhyme-spitter who fluidly shifts from hard-core grit to Barbie-doll cute. She's been featured on dozens of rap and R & B tracks, and she's the only femcee [female MC] currently on the rap charts.

Her long-anticipated debut, *Pink Friday*, has two missions: Cement Minaj's stardom and, perhaps, wedge the door open a little wider for more female rappers. *Friday* gets it about half right. There's enough pop ear candy to ensure that she'll stick around, but she's probably got more work to do to win over doubtful hip-hop heads.

The way she roars out of the box with the swaggering "I'm the Best" and the ferocious "Roman's Revenge" featuring Eminem, it seems that she'll cater mostly to fans of her rawer style. But it's her army of pop-leaning Barbies and Kens that will come away most satisfied.

It's the emotional, radio-friendly tracks such as "Save Me," "Right Thru Me" and "Fly," which features Rihanna, that dominate the album.

—Steve Jones

Released in May 2011, the song peaked at No. 3 on the *Billboard* Hot 100 chart. It also hit No. 8 on the U.K. Singles Chart. In March 2012, "Super Bass" was certified quadruple-platinum by the RIAA. It had sold more than four million digital copies, the first song by a female rapper to reach sales of that magnitude.

Roman Meets Slim Shady

All along, Nicki had always wanted to work with rapper Eminem, whom she views as a legend. After talking about it for a long time, she plucked up her courage to ask him. She sent him an invitation to record together, along with a song she thought could use a guest feature. Eminem responded that the track wasn't really his style. Nicki did have another track, produced by a hip-hop producer called Swizz Beatz. The song featured a repeating line snipped from the song "Scenario" by A Tribe Called Quest. Nicki knew the track was good and had intended the song to be a solo.

After thinking it over, she sent the track to Eminem. She was nervous that he might reject her a second time. Nicki was ecstatic to get a call from Eminem saying he was in. The result of the collaboration was "Roman's Revenge." For the song, Nicki rapped as her alter ego Roman, and Eminem channeled his perverse Slim Shady persona.

The two characters exchange foulmouthed verses about their twisted minds. Slim makes disparaging remarks about homosexuals and talks about hurting women. Roman boasts that he is superior to other rappers. At the end of the song, the Martha character warns the pair

Working with a legend: At the 2011 Grammys, Nicki presents legendary rapper Eminem with his award for Best Rap Solo Performance. The next year, the two collaborated on Nicki's song "Roman's Revenge."

that they will be locked up in jail. She also tells them they should wash their mouths out with soap because of their crude language.

Many listeners saw the song as a dig at Lil' Kim, a female rapper who has publicly accused Nicki of copying her style. Roman talks about a "has-been" and claims that the person in question is angry because Nicki has taken her spot at the top of the female rap world.

IN F○CUS

Singles, Albums, and Digital Downloads

In the music industry, a single is typically a single track or song released for sale or free of charge to the public. Singles used to be released on vinyl but are most often available to be downloaded digitally. Albums are collections of songs by a recording artist or band and can be released as vinyl, a compact disc, or a digital download. A digital download is the process of downloading music from the Internet or a website to a user's computer or phone.

Singles are often what the record label or artist considers to be the most popular songs from an album. They're released ahead of an album for commercial use on radio to build up demand and interest in the album.

Fans of the song can also download a copy of their favorite single without having to invest in the whole album. Singles can also be distributed after the release of an album to keep up awareness and drive further sales of individual tracks as well as the collection.

Sometimes singles can be released that don't make it onto the album. Often this is because they didn't sell as well as expected or because they were considered promotional only—that is, they were designed to create attention but not for inclusion on the album. Sometimes if singles released ahead of an album sell poorly, the record label can decide not to release an album at all.

The song was released exclusively through iTunes (Apple's online music store) and made it to No. 57 on the *Billboard* Hot 100. A remix featuring verses by Lil Wayne was released a few months later. Rapper Buster Rhymes, from A Tribe Called Quest, also created a remix.

We Came to Win

The final single to be released from *Pink Friday* was "Fly," an inspirational song that Nicki cowrote. The lyrics examine her attempts to rise above criticism, to overcome obstacles, and to thrive in the tough entertainment industry. The producer of the track, J.R. Rotem, recalls that the first version they created used a studio session singer for the chorus. Nicki was excited about the song but wanted to replace the

singer with Rihanna. At the time, Rihanna was extremely busy recording and touring. J. R. warned Nicki that she shouldn't get her hopes up. Afterward, he said it was a sign of Nicki's star power that Rihanna agreed to do the track.

On her Facebook page, Nicki told fans that "Fly" was one of her absolute favorite songs on the album. She described it as a song of empowerment and about flying in the face of adversity. Released in August 2011, the song reached No. 19 on the *Billboard* Hot 100, becoming the fourth Top 20 hit on the charts from *Pink Friday*.

On the fly: Rihanna *(above)* recorded the chorus track for Nicki's single "Fly," released in 2011. Rihanna is originally from Barbados, an island nation about 250 miles (400 kilometers) from Nicki's homeland of Trinidad.

It reached No. 16 on the U.K. Singles Chart, making it Nicki's fifth Top 30 Single in the United Kingdom.

Nicki crowned the year 2011 by accepting an invitation to open the American Music Awards on November 20, 2011. On the night of the show, Nicki freaked out just moments before her performance. She says, "I had a horrible malfunction with the clothes and the hair ten minutes before I opened. So I was backstage having a . . . nervous breakdown . . . My hair was supposed to light up, my choker was too small. So while I was in the box, waiting for the show to open, I had to rip the [stuff] off, throw it to the side, and act like nothing happened. When I got offstage I freaked out because it was just so emotional. I really, really, really wanted that to be a [good] show."

Nicki's outfit included aluminum chaps, clocks on her chest, and speakers on her backside. Despite her backstage fears, she gave high-energy renditions of "Turn Me On" and "Super Bass," complete with fireworks and smoke-spewing robots on stilts. To cap her achievement, she took home the honors for Best Rap Artist of the Year. And her album *Pink Friday* even beat out Lil Wayne's *Tha Carter IV* for Best Hip-Hop Album of the Year. *Pink Friday* was a certified hit. By early 2012, the album had sold more than 1.7 million copies.

Super Bowl Superstar

Nicki continued to break new ground, shattering Music Choice's video on demand (VOD) record for the most single week views for a music video in history. The "Super Bass" music video received 1.4 million views for the week ending May 29, 2011. This was the largest number ever recorded for one single week since Music Choice VOD launched in November 2004. By November 2011, Nicki held three of the top five spots.

In December 2011, Madonna posted on her Facebook page that she was looking for people to collaborate with her on an upcoming album. Soon afterward, she announced she was teaming up with Nicki and English recording artist M.I.A. on a dance-pop track called "Give Me

IN FOCUS

Music Choice Video On Demand : Top Five Spots (November 2011)

1. Nicki Minaj's "Super Bass" 1,436,807 views for week ending May 29, 2011
2. Nicki Minaj's "Right Thru Me" 1,278,807 views for week ending November 10, 2010
3. Justin Bieber's "Baby" 1,222,670 views for week ending April 4, 2010
4. Lil Wayne's "Lollipop" 1,180,360 views for week ending April 13, 2008
5. Nicki Minaj's "Your Love" 1,062,915 views for week ending August 15, 2010

All Your Luvin'". In interviews Madonna praised both young women for their independence and unconventionality. The three worked on verses and a video clip. The clip features a sports theme with Nicki and M.I.A. dressed as cheerleaders. Football players carry Madonna. The goofy video also includes the three women dressed as Marilyn Monroe in white dresses and platinum wigs.

The reason for the sports theme soon became clear. The Super Bowl announced its lineup for the halftime show. Madonna was the lead act. She invited electropop duo LMFAO, singer-songwriter Cee Lo Green, Nicki, and M.I.A. to join her. The "Luvin'" single was released as the first track from Madonna's *MDNA* album on February 3, 2012, two days before the Super Bowl. The song peaked at No. 10 on the *Billboard* Hot 100 and reached No. 1 on the *Billboard* Hot Dance Club Songs chart.

For the halftime show, Madonna dressed in Cleopatra style and

Super Bowl dream: Nicki and M.I.A. *(right)* put on cheerleader garb to perform with pop megastar Madonna *(center)* at the Super Bowl halftime show in February 2012.

was carried into the Super Bowl stadium by men dressed as gladiators. She sang "Vogue" and "Music" and was then joined by LMFAO for "Party Rock Anthem" and "Sexy and I Know It." Nicki and M.I.A. wore Egyptian-style headpieces atop leather, military-style cheerleader outfits. They performed "Give Me All Your Luvin'" among a group of cheerleaders. The halftime act also featured Cirque du Soleil performers, several drumlines, and a 200-person choir. The over-the-top spectacle was viewed by more than 114 million people, making it the most watched Super Bowl halftime show ever.

Nicki was over the moon to be invited to collaborate with Madonna. Nicki says working with her changed her life. Watching her icon rehearse for the Super Bowl over and over, long after the crew thought things were perfect, inspired Nicki to work harder than ever. Nicki was extremely proud of the performance.

Nicki says of the experience, "It does feel like every moment is getting bigger and bigger. Not only did I get a call to do a song with Madonna, but then I got a call to do a video with Madonna, and then— oh, by the way—you're going to do the Super Bowl with Madonna. This is not really happening!"

Stand Alone Stand Out

As Nicki's career took off, she didn't really take time to smell the roses. She was continually focused on what was next. And what was next was writing new songs, working on new beats, and mixing and producing her next album. She was also aware that many of the big moments in her career had not been hers alone. Joining the Young Money crew, she'd wanted to prove she could stand apart from Lil Wayne. And some of her biggest songs since then were with big names such as Drake and Eminem. Nicki was on a quest to be recognized for standing on her own.

Her focus was on her solo set for the 54th Grammy ceremony, scheduled for February 12, 2012. This would be the first time the Grammy stage had ever hosted a solo female rapper. Her spectacular piece, dubbed *The Exorcism of Roman*, was set to a song called "Roman Holiday." The song would be the first track on her new album, *Pink Friday: Roman Reloaded*. The song and the stage performance are about an exorcism (a religious practice to rid a person of demons). The set was the interior of a cathedral, complete with floor-to-ceiling stained-glass windows. Nicki plays a sweet, innocent woman possessed by her outspoken alter ego Roman. Her mother invites a priest to rid Nicki of Roman. The exorcism takes place in the cathedral, amidst dancing hooded figures and plumes of fire and smoke.

February 13, 2012

Nicki Minaj's 'Exorcism' Riles Grammy Viewers

From the Pages of
USA TODAY

And the Grammy Award for most polarizing performance at Sunday's show goes to . . . Nicki Minaj!

Fox News writes that her levitating act with religious messages was so "20 years ago" when Madonna did it. And then Gaga resurrected it, so to speak, two years ago [in her "Judas" video].

Minaj got the party started when she arrived on the red carpet channeling her Roman Zolanski alter ego in a little red riding hood outfit that was said to be a Versace nun-inspired satin robe. Her "date" was a man who resembled the pope.

On stage, she debuted her new song, "Roman Holiday," by performing an onstage exorcism, seemingly on herself, complete with levitation, stained glass, lighting and gibberish. As a white-hooded church choir sang, Minaj strapped herself to a leather table and was lifted into the air, flames burning beneath her.

The mood backstage was a mixture of confusion, embarrassment and offense as the performance dragged on, going deeper and deeper in mocking Catholic faith, reports Fox News.

While many on Twitter applauded her performance, others slammed it.

Tweeted *The View*'s Sherri Shepherd: "Watching Nicki Minaj . . . I didn't know whether to dance or pull out my Bible and lay hands on the tv . . . 2 old for the #Grammys. . . ."

—Ann Oldenburg/Lifeline Live

Controversial entrance: Nicki arrived at the Grammy Awards in 2012 with a companion dressed as the pope, the leader of the worldwide Catholic Church. Some people felt the choice was disrespectful to the church.

But the priest is not successful, and Roman refuses to be banished. At the end of the set, Nicki's character rises far above the stage, in triumph.

Viewer reaction ranged from shocked to thrilled to bored. But the piece got people talking. For example, the Catholic League—a Roman Catholic advocacy organization—condemned the piece, feeling it mocked the Catholic religion. Nicki herself was delighted with how it turned out. She credited creative director Laurieann Gibson for

On a high: Nicki rises above the stage at the end of her performance of "Roman Holiday" at the 2012 Grammys.

its theatricality. She says the song is a theatrical piece, not a club song. She doesn't care if people outside her Barbz don't understand it. She was proud of the performance, which she felt was her best to date.

Crazy energy: Nicki describes her alter ego Roman Zolanski as a crazy, violent, male force who lives within her. Here, she channels Roman at the 2012 Grammys.

Alter Egos

Pink Friday showed that Nicki was a versatile force to be reckoned with. The album also allowed her to introduce a number of alter egos. For example, the song "Roman's Revenge" featured the characters Roman Zolanski and Martha. Nicki describes Roman as an angry, vicious, crazy, flamboyant boy. Martha is his British mom. Other songs on the album feature Nicki's Barbie character. Modeled after the Barbie doll, this character is soft-spoken and childlike. Nicki's verses on Trey Songz "Bottoms Up" feature Roman rapping about his Louisville slugger baseball bat. Barbie then makes an appearance with sing-song lines including a mention of babies in Haiti.

One of the bonus tracks on the deluxe edition of *Roman Reloaded* is "Press Conference." It is a sit-down interview with radio personality Charlemagne Tha God. Nicki tells him that when she first got into the music business, people wanted her to be a one-dimensional, sex kitten, female rapper. With her success, she can display all aspects of her personality. As someone with a passion for acting, Nicki loves the theatrical side of entertaining. "When I started winning, I started feeling that I can be myself. I can do my accents, I can do my voices, I can do my faces, I can do costumes. . . . I can now really bring me into it. And I think . . . that people thought that when I first came out, that that was me in my entirety. But that wasn't. That was a small facet of who I was. But, who you see now is a more multi-faceted mixture of all the different personalities that I have in me."

Nicki says playing different characters allows her to have fun and not take herself so seriously. After all those years playing roles

Costume fashion: Nicki's Barbie character is inspired by cosplay, the costume-based style of Japanese Harajuku fashion. Pink is her signature color.

at drama school, it felt natural for her to create new characters. After being told for years what a female rapper should look or act like, she was ready to experiment and push the boundaries. Female rappers had typically fallen into two camps. Either you had to dress like an urban male in hoodies, slouched hat and sneakers, or you were expected to look like a sex object. You could mix it up between the two, but there seemed to be no middle ground.

Nicki reveals, "After a certain amount of time of feeling really boxed in, I decided I wanted to be crazy, I wanted to be out of the box and I wanted to sort of dare to be different. So then I started exploring, with accents and crazy voices and all this great stuff that really gives me life . . . it makes a dull little girl become a crazy, wonderful, iconic person, so that's what I've been working towards." She says that even the character the world knows as Nicki Minaj is a sort of alter ego. The fierce, no-nonsense rapper is a star created and played by Onika Maraj. She says it's all just one big theater piece.

Shape-Shifter

Nicki explains that her characters reflect the different people she has to be in real life. For example, she likes to be sweet and nurturing to her fans. But she can't be like that in a business situation. There, she's a businesswoman negotiating tough deals and she needs to be assertive. With her staff, she needs to act like a boss, not like a little girl. Nicki has observed that when men are direct and commanding, people view them as leaders and "bossed up" (powerful and important). On the other hand, when women act the same way, people view them negatively. Nicki's song "Dear Old Nicki" shows the tough spot she's in. She sings and raps about how some fans want to see the soft, innocent Nicki from earlier in her career. They accuse her of having become too hard and too mainstream. Nicki attributes the change to getting older and being in the business longer. She says she feels like an older sister to the "old Nicki."

Nicki recognizes that some hip-hop traditionalists don't like her

Fuzzy: Nicki out and about in London, England, in 2012 wearing one of her quirky outfits. Nicki doesn't care if people in the industry don't understand her style. She enjoys expressing her personality through her outfits.

theatrical side. "When I started making those weird voices, a lot of [record industry] people told me how whack it was," she says. 'What . . . are you doing?' they'd say. 'Why do you sound like that? That doesn't sound sexy to me.' And then I started saying, Oh, that's not sexy to you? Good. I'm going to do it more. Maybe I don't want to be sexy to you today. . . . I never thought in a million years that it would mean more people would start listening to my music," she says.

She says she doesn't care if industry executives think she's weird or don't understand her style. She's happy to express who she is and be herself. She realizes that by expressing all of her personality, she can reach people who would never have listened to a female rapper. She also understands that she's never really going to be able to predict what appeals to an audience and what won't. For example, in 2010, MTV released the documentary *Nicki Minaj: My Time Now*. In one scene, Nicki tears up as she talks about the death of her grandmother.

After filming that scene, Nicki lost sleep. She worried about having shown the real person behind the glamorous façade. She feared that viewers would be disappointed to discover that she was human. Instead, she received many compliments—and new fans.

Beyond the Urban Audience

Nicki has discovered that her different personalities resonate with different audiences. For example, after *Pink Friday*'s release, Nicki toured with Lil Wayne. The people in that audience were urban, male, hip-hop fans. But when she joined Britney Spears' Femme Fatale Tour as the opening act in 2011, she drew a very different crowd. Not only did young female fans come to see her, but gay male admirers showed up as well. Many of Nicki's gay fans love her exaggerated, drag-style costumes and her theatricality. Hip-hop has not traditionally welcomed women or gay people. Nicki says she relates to her gay fans as fellow outsiders.

Team player: Nicki performed with pop sensation Britney Spears *(left)* at the Billboard Music Awards in May 2011, just before joining Britney's Femme Fatale Tour.

Mini me: *From left:* Young fans Sophia Grace Brownlee and her cousin Rosie McClellan join Nicki in singing "Super Bass" onstage as Ellen watches during the *Ellen DeGeneres Show* in 2011.

As the more pop-oriented songs gained radio airplay, Nicki was surprised to find that she was attracting very young female fans. They like the dress-up aspects of her look and her cartoonish voices. She says she makes sure to release clean versions of her adult songs for these young fans. Two of her young British fans—eight-year-old Sophia Grace Brownlee and her five-year-old cousin Rosie McClellan—posted a homemade video of the two of them singing Nicki's hit "Super Bass." The video went viral, attracting 11 million hits and landing the little girls an appearance on the *Ellen DeGeneres Show*. Ellen invited Nicki to phone in to the show. Instead, Nicki rearranged her schedule so she could be there in person. The audience loved Sophia Grace and Rosie's rendition of the song. The girls put on blond-pink wigs and completely nailed the difficult rap. And when Nicki came onstage to meet the girls, Sophia Grace screamed with excitement and threw herself into Nicki's arms. Then the three of them performed the song together.

Nicki Minaj Brings Her Theatrical Style to *Pink Friday* [Excerpt 2]

<u>From the Pages of</u>
<u>USA TODAY</u>

Nicki Minaj channels the acting skills she developed (in high school) and her lingering [worries] into the characters whose voices she affects. "When I was little, my mother and I would speak in all these different accents, just for fun. And I would watch movies over and over, literally hundreds of times, to master whatever accent they were doing. And I took a special liking to British accents."

Hence "Roman Zolanski" . . . who appears on *Pink Friday*, going one on one with Eminem's Slim Shady on the track *Roman's Revenge*. "Roman is my wicked alter ego," Minaj explains. "He's English. He tells it like it is, doesn't care what you think, isn't trying to please you."

[Another alter ego] "Barbie," who appears elsewhere on the album, is "more soft-spoken and sweet. She sounds like a character in a fairy tale."

Minaj laughs, then pauses. "Maybe I'm afraid or ashamed to say or do certain things, or I don't want to deal with the backlash. You can always create other people—though I don't really create them. It's not a conscious decision. I'll just go into the studio and hear a voice. If I keep hearing that same voice, then I'll name the person."

Tour in the works

The "regular Nicki Minaj" is "more the traditional New York rap chick"—even if she doesn't call New York home at the moment. "I'm based in Los Angeles now, and though I know New Yorkers will hate me for saying this, it's been a refreshing change. It's warmer, a little friendlier, and I feel less pressure in L.A. I can go out [dressed] very low-key and no one pays me any mind."

If Minaj values her privacy, she is hardly shy in discussing certain personal inclinations. Courting yet more comparisons with that other pop provocateur [Lady Gaga], she speaks proudly of her substantial gay following. "I'm not gay," she says.

Look-alikes: Fans dress up at an autograph signing in New York after the release of Nicki's first album, *Pink Friday*.

"But I do love women, and the way I speak about women and treat my female fans is very abnormal. I'll reference a girl having a beautiful [behind] or beautiful [breasts]. I'll kiss my fans, let them touch me. But do I go home with them at night?. . . No."

Minaj, who says she isn't dating anyone right now, does "feel a weird sense of connection to my gay fans. I identify with them, because people have also looked at me like I'm peculiar. And a few people in the media have made fun of me, said some really mean things. So I know what it's like to be tormented for wanting to express yourself. I don't go out of my way to treat gay fans like they're special; I just see them as people who love and who want to have fun."

The next item on Minaj's agenda is a tour, on which she hopes to get closer to all her fans, in all respects. "That's a big deal for me. I don't want to give too much away yet, but at the top of the year, we'll announce plans. And we'll be going everywhere."

Live performance is, after all, "another form of escape, of transition," Minaj says. "It's all about constant transformation, about never looking the same or talking the same or acting the same. You have to always keep people guessing."

—Elysa Gardner

Since Nicki has so many young fans, she has reconsidered the raw sexiness in her songs. She says her crew teases her about new lyrics, asking, "Could Sophia Grace sing that?" For this reason, she decided to lessen some of the sexual content. Nicki says, "I made a conscious decision to try to tone down the sexiness. I want people—especially young girls—to know that in life, nothing is going to be based on sex appeal. You've got to have something else to go with that."

Still, she does retain adult themes for her older fans. Many of them love the shock value of her lyrics. Even celebrities have become fans, with stars such as Grammy-winning Taylor Swift and teen pop idol Selena Gomez recording versions of "Super Bass" on YouTube and performing the song in concert.

Inspiring women: Rappers Missy Elliott *(left)* and Lauryn Hill *(right)* respect Nicki's work. Nicki points to the two women as inspirations for her own career.

Nicki is a fan of women performers too. She openly admires strong women. She has publicly thanked women rappers such as Missy Elliot and Lauryn Hill for inspiring her. She still finds it hard to believe that she got to make a video with Mariah Carey, and she idolizes Madonna. Nicki has spoken publicly about her awe of Madonna's ability to entertain, make music, and successfully mix business success with raising a family.

Mixing it up: Nicki loves to blend crazy, colorful outfits with her natural sexiness to create a unique look.

Fashion Alert

Before Nicki was famous, many people had encouraged her to use her curvaceous body and her sex appeal to get ahead in the music industry. But when she met Lil Wayne, he encouraged Nicki to be true to her quirky self. He himself is no stranger to freakiness. He sports diamond teeth and a tattooed face. Nicki remembers, "Before I met Wayne, the person that was spearheading my career [at the time] was the one person who always told me, 'Don't be too playful, don't be too kooky and weird . . . no one's gonna feel that, nobody wants to hear that.' So I stifled a lot of that early on, and then once we parted ways, I was like, 'Guess what, I'm gonna just be me.'"

Early Attitude

Even as a child, Nicki had an interest in fashion and hair. Fashion was a great distraction from her rough home life. She was obsessed with the color pink and trying out new looks. About her hair, she remembers that when she was nine years old, "I was doing every- and anything to it—putting in wads of gel and brushing it to the next century, and just thinking I was so cute. I always thought I had an eye for that stuff . . . [and one time] I had done something I thought was really, really, really cute, and I showed my neighbor. She was like, 'Why'd you do that to your hair?' And I never forget what I said: 'I'm someone new in this hair.'"

She says she was always getting new cornrow holders for her hair and tweaking and perming it. Once, when she was fourteen, she wanted to get blond highlights, but the hairdresser refused. Nicki said she was crying and begging, but the stylist wouldn't budge unless she got her mom on the phone to give permission. She says she was always experimental. In fact, Nicki says that Cyndi Lauper's fun fashions and

Sisters in fashion: At her peak in the 1980s, pop star Cyndi Lauper *(above, in 1983)* fashioned a look that Nicki points to as an inspiration for her own quirky sense of style.

February 13, 2011

Nicki Minaj's Grammy outfit: 'Fabulocity meets fashionista'

<u>From the Pages of</u>
<u>USA TODAY</u>

Nicki Minaj looked purrrr-fectly wild on the Grammy red carpet.

"This outfit is a masterpiece by Givenchy," declared the singer.

"And what they made for me is a miraculous piece of lionesss-meets-her-cub-meets-fabulocity-meets-fashionista-meets-runaway-meets-everything," she told Ryan Seacrest.

—Ann Oldenburg

Roar: Nicki wears a Givenchy-inspired animal-print outfit on the Grammy red carpet.

hairdos in her music videos were a great inspiration to Nicki's own sense of fashion.

As an adult, Nicki has become more fearless in her fashion choices. She told *Teen Vogue* that she loves off-the-wall, radical, colorful pieces. "You should never feel afraid to become a piece of art. It's exhilarating." When asked if she'd ever regretted an outfit after wearing it, Nicki laughs. "All the time, but it's the price you pay when you wanna play!" She says her favorite fashion item is flat knee-high boots. "They can be cheap or expensive, purple, green, yellow, pink—you name it. I'm in heels a lot, so I love when I can slip my boots on. They're comfortable and so cute!" For heels, she's crazy about the colorful, and expensive, shoes by French designer Christian Louboutin.

Slip

Nicki says her wigs and fashion outfits allow her to show off her fun side. While offstage, she often has to be a boss and a businesswoman. She would actually prefer to be girlie and play dress up. She does that away from the board-room table. The ability to reinvent herself through hair and fashion has ensured that Nicki is always in the news. However, she received more exposure than she wanted during a live performance on *Good Morning America* in August 2011. For that appearance, Nicki wore an umbrella-like see-through vinyl skirt with pink edging and a matching jacket. She paired it with leggings printed with a comic-strip motif and a small green crop top. During her energetic dancing, her nipple briefly

Oops: Nicki's outfit on the *Good Morning America* show in August 2011 caused an embarrassing moment in which she accidentally exposed some chest flesh during her live performance.

rose up and out of her top. Nicki was upset. Visibly embarrassed, she later apologized on the late-night news show *Nightline*, stressing that the slip was definitely not something she would ever do on purpose.

I'm Really Sitting with Anna!

Nicki credits a number of women as her style idols. They include singers Janet Jackson ("sexy, strong mysterious"), Cyndi Lauper ("eye-catching, colorful"), and Salt-n-Pepa (for their bangs) . Nicki also admires model Naomi Campbell ("fierce") and legendary Hollywood actress Marilyn Monroe ("the epitome of sexy Hollywood glam"). Nicki loves to take inspiration from all these women for her own sexy, colorful, kooky ensembles.

Happy Birthday: Nicki *(center)* celebrated her twenty-eighth birthday in Las Vegas. Seated to her right is model-actress Amber Rose.

Nicki says she gets bored easily. One way to avoid boredom is to constantly change her look. One of Nicki's memorable outfits was a dramatic orange-pink dress with a flexible gold metallic frame by Indian designer Manish Arora (see page 3). She wore the spectacular dress to the 2010 American Music Awards. Pairing the dress with jewel-decorated Louboutin open-toed heels and green-tipped hair, Nicki made a splash. For another event—to celebrate her birthday in December 2010—Nicki headed for TAO, a nightclub in Las Vegas. She chose a pearl-embellished nude bodysuit, shimmery heels, and a coordinating long blond wig with bangs. And at the 2011 MTV Video Music Awards, Nicki wore a gown with a mirrored top and tutu skirt. On her face, she had a cartooned surgical-style face mask. For her feet, she chose fuzzy slippers. The entire outfit was capped off with a blond, pink, and yellow hair knot.

Nicki loves to go to fashion shows too. The paparazzi (journalists who chase stars for photos) are crazy for Nicki's outfits. For example, she wore a gorgeous green and black Oscar

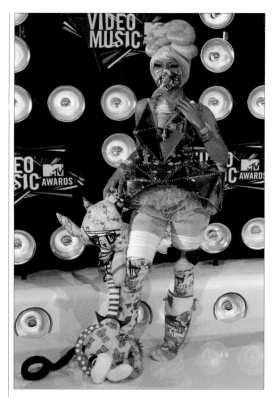

Toyland costume: Nicki's outfit for the 2011 MTV Video Music Awards baffled many people. For example, a journalist for the Internet newspaper the *Huffington Post* humorously suggested the star got her outfit at Toys "R" Us.

de la Renta dress with a lacy black camisole top and a full green skirt to the 2011 American Music Awards. She hit the stage in a towering pair of Alexander McQueen armor wedge sandals that proved difficult to walk in. She almost fell a couple of times as she made her way to the microphone. The McQueen sandals feature a molded metal heel and cost a staggering $4,250. After her speeches at the award ceremony, Nicki chose a more comfortable pair of shoes—sneakers.

For the launch of designer Carolina Herrera's Spring 2012 collection, Nicki wore a very playful outfit. The central piece was a neon orange pleated tennis skirt and green net leggings over hot pink tights. On top she wore a sleeveless vest of multicolored pompoms. To top it all off,

Walking in style: Nicki wore these armor wedge platform sandals by Alexander McQueen to the 2011 American Music Awards.

Twins: *Vogue* editor Anna Wintour *(center)* joked with Nicki about their matching outfits at this fashion show in New York in 2011.

IN FOCUS

Anna Wintour

Anna Wintour is the editor in chief of American *Vogue*. Born in England in 1949, Wintour worked in fashion before becoming a journalist. She wrote first at *Harpers Bazaar* and then worked for the weekly pop culture magazine *New York*. Eventually she became creative director for American *Vogue* and editor of British *Vogue*. Wintour achieved her dream of editorship of American *Vogue* in 1988. Known for being aloof and demanding, she has been criticized as difficult to work for. All the same, many people praise her eye for fashion and her support of new and up-coming designers.

With her signature bob haircut and dark sunglasses, Wintour is one of the most influential people in fashion in the United States. Her power includes deciding what is seen (and not seen) in *Vogue*, setting trends, and recommending designers for fashion houses. Her famous guests at fashion shows have included singer Taylor Swift, New York senator Kirsten Gillibrand, and Amar'e Stoudemire of the New York Knicks.

Nicki did her hair in a tall blond beehive. At this show, Nicki was the guest of Anna Wintour, influential editor-in-chief of American *Vogue*. The next day, Nicki was surprised to receive an autographed snapshot from Anna of the two women at the show. The caption of the photo read, "We match!" In contrast to Nicki's bold style, Anna's look was very simple and elegant. But Anna's chic orange and black print dress did match the orange in Nicki's skirt and in her black and orange heels. Nicki was touched by the gesture. She planned to put the photo in her gym to inspire her workouts.

Nicki chose a more subdued look to join Anna in the front row at designer Oscar de la Renta's Spring 2012 show. Subdued for Nicki, that is. The rapper came as Barbie, wearing a leopard print leotard

Japanese style: The colorful street fashions *(above)* worn by young people in the Harajuku area of Tokyo, Japan, have inspired fashion designers all over the world. Nicki models many of her fashion choices after the Harajuku style.

over black tights with a child's plush tiger hat and leopard print short boots. Even her hair had leopard spots! Nicki mentioned Anna in the song "Muny" from the deluxe version of *Pink Friday*. She pretends she's talking to Anna and says she wants to be on *Vogue*'s front cover. She also lists some of her favorite fashion brands including Versace, Louis Vuitton, Chanel, Vanson, and Gucci.

After these shows though, Nicki confessed that she likes street fashion in Tokyo, Japan, better than runway fashion in the United States and Europe. She admires the way Japanese teens ignore fashion norms and combine things that don't look like they match yet somehow always look right.

Gettin' Wiggy

Eye-catching wigs adorn all of Nicki's attention-getting outfits. She loves everything from platinum blond tresses to towering pastel Marge Simpson beehives. Nicki matches her hair to her outfit, her mood, or sometimes just to the occasion. For example, Nicki wore a green wig for a charity event benefiting green organizations. For the 2011 Grammys, she sported leopard print bangs to match her leopard print dress. She says the ever-changing sizes, colors, and styles of her hair make her feel as if she can be a different person every day. However, she does admit the wigs can be difficult to travel with! Each one has its own box and takes up a lot of space.

Nicki has her own hairstylist—Terrence Davidson. He keeps Nicki's wigs on shelves in a bedroom of his home. He jokes that it's about time the wigs started paying rent. Nicki has hundreds of wigs, including multiples of her blond and black bobs. Terrence hand assembles, styles, and dyes all of Nicki's wigs. They are made of real human hair. Real hair in wigs is an advantage because it can be curled. Synthetic hair can't.

Nicki's natural hair is black. But she says it's too much work to curl or flat iron her own hair for the different styles she needs for all the events she attends.

Wiggy: Nicki loves to wear elaborate hairpieces and wigs. She wore this pink wig while making stops at radio stations in London, England.

March 30, 2011

Nicki Minaj Goes Green for Eco-auction

From the Pages of
USA TODAY

Nicki Minaj always knows the right thing to wear. She dyed half her hair green to perform at last night's

Green Auction: Bid to Save the Earth at Christie's in New York.

All proceeds from the auction and green fashion show will go to science-based non-profits including Oceana, the Natural Resources Defense Council, Conservation International and the Central Park Conservancy.

As for the rumors that she had turned down an offer to judge the new *X Factor* show, Minaj told reporters, "I can't talk about that, but I love Simon [Cowell] very dearly. He's such an amazing man. I had the pleasure of meeting him and my life will never be the same, darling. I told him that. I was absolutely in love with him prior to meeting him. And now that I've met him, it's like I dream about him every night."

—Ann Oldenburg/Lifeline Live

Green hair: Nicki's green wig fit the bill for the eco-auction she attended in New York in 2011.

Wigs are much more convenient. The ability to curl them in advance shaves a lot of time off the preparation for each outfit. For an *Allure* magazine cover shoot, Nicki wore a huge mass of fuchsia curls that required two days and five hairpieces to create. There's no way Terrence could have worked on Nicki's real hair for that long! For the cover, she was dressed to look like French queen Marie Antoinette (1755–1793). The queen would have been envious!

Lips and lashes: Nicki's recognizable look includes superlong lashes and her pouty pink lips.

Nicki is also well known for her signature pink lips and cartoonishly long eyelashes. Without the lashes, she says she feels naked. Nicki says she doesn't have the patience or steady hands to do her own lashes. She absolutely needs her makeup artist to do them. She also relies on her makeup artist to do her brows and to color her eyelids.

Daring to Be Different

Nicki's alter egos have their own looks too. She says that if she's wearing her own black hair and is dressed down, that's the Nicki character. Roman is more outlandish, wearing speakers on his backside. Barbie usually wears little dresses and the Barbie necklace.

Some people feel Nicki is an exhibitionist, who likes to show herself off. Others see her avant-garde outfits as a necessary way to stay

USA TODAY

Life

SECTION D

LIFE.USATODAY.COM

November 23, 2010

Nicki Minaj Brings Her Theatrical Style to *Pink Friday* [Excerpt 3]

From the Pages of

USA TODAY

Before you judge Nicki Minaj, try walking a mile in her shoes. But first, make sure you have access to a good chiropractor.

Hip-hop's hottest new star... turns up at her record company offices in diamond-studded, razor-thin Balenciaga stilettos. "They're about 3 inches [7.6 centimeters]," Minaj estimates. "Which is modest."

On her legs, Minaj wears a black "strappy contraption" stretched over cotton-candy-colored tights that match the pink tips of her long, platinum-blond wig. It's exactly the kind of ensemble you'd expect from the woman *Billboard* recently dubbed "The First Lady (Gaga) of Hip-Hop."

Minaj, 25, has mixed feelings about the Gaga reference. "Every artist wants to be recognized as an individual," she says. "On the other hand, I'm being compared to a world-freaking-wide superstar. And I love her—love her music, her boldness, her fearlessness. I love all women who take charge."

"My look is an extension of everything I do," she says. "Nobody talks about Nicki Minaj without talking about 'the look.' I don't know if that's a good thing or a bad thing, but I like to keep people entertained—and I think you should be entertaining from your head to your toes."

—Elysa Gardner

in the spotlight. Nicki claims otherwise. Offstage, she's a completely different person. "I'm the biggest homebody. But I've [always] been like this. Nothing about me has changed since I got fame. I never liked to go to clubs. I never liked to go out. I don't know where that public craziness came from. I was always like a comedian to my friends and family, but in a lot of ways I'm shy." Still, she does get excited about eccentric getups. She laughs, knowing that most people wouldn't have the courage to wear what she does.

In a lot of ways, Nicki's unconventional outfits are just part of the brand identity the rapper has created for herself. At home and in the studio, she wears sweatpants and T-shirts. But when she goes out in public, she knows fans expect something special. They want to know that she has made an effort. She feels the fans are consumers of her business. They deserve a little moment of excitement or fantasy as they glimpse their star in person or in paparazzi shots. She says, "I work well with people who

Queen of fashion: Nicki keeps her fans guessing about what she'll wear next. Here she poses after winning her Best Female Hip-Hop Artist award at the BET Awards in July 2012.

trust my instinct and understand that I am the marketer and promoter of the Nicki Minaj brand. This did not come overnight. This did not happen from a record company. No manager created this." And so far, her instincts are proving to be right. Her brand and her albums are runaway successes.

NICKI MINAJ *Pink* FRIDAY ROMAN RELOADED

PAREN
ADVIS
EXPLICIT C

Cover magic: Nicki looks tough on the cover of her second album, *Pink Friday: Roman Reloaded*. The album is a mix of fun hip-hop and dance-pop tunes.

Roman Reloaded

Fans were excited to see what Nicki would produce on her second album. She promised lots more of Roman and her other alter egos along with the old, fierce Nicki and the new, pop Nicki. Describing *Pink Friday: Roman Reloaded*, Nicki said, "I've never had this much fun recording music in my life. My first album . . . I felt like I was making music to please everyone else. I had to be politically correct, but this album I am just creating music, and there's such a big difference. Literally in the studio we were cracking up laughing, having fun, and enjoying ourselves. The music itself you're going to get every side that I've ever shown and then a little bit extra. . . . I've tried to make it very, very balanced, because I don't ever want to be boxed in, and that's always what drives me. So I made a very diverse album."

She added that with her first album, she "was a too open Nicki Minaj. It felt more to me like a diary, the songs were more introspective . . . with this particular album I felt that it was time to give people a moment to enjoy the lyrics, and enjoy the beats, and enjoy the voices. . . . I made it my business to make an album that did not talk about sex at all. With this album I'm going back to . . . the feeling of 'I don't care what you think!' That's what it is."

Hits and Misses

In December 2011, Nicki released a promotional single called "Roman in Moscow." She described the song as a teaser, like a trailer for a movie that would give fans a feel for the album. Sung from the point of view of Roman, the song didn't chart well and was not included on the album. Two weeks after the release of "Roman in Moscow," the promotional track "Stupid H—" came out. Black Entertainment Television banned the video on its channel without citing reasons. Nicki tweeted to fans that they should watch the video on VEVO. She didn't want the

VEVO video: Nicki directed fans to VEVO to watch her "Stupid H—" video. In the video, she sports a range of wigs and makeup, including long black hair and blue face paint.

video to premiere on a network where it could be tampered with or compromised. The video set a record by accumulating 4.8 million views during its first twenty-four hours online.

Nicki claims the song is about "all haters." Yet it is widely seen as a response to rapper Lil' Kim. Lil' Kim had recorded a song about Nicki called "Black Friday." In the song, she charges Nicki with being a poor imitation of the Queen Bee (Lil' Kim). In "Stupid H—" Nicki answers back in terms that imply fans have chosen her over Kim.

In a collaborative move, French DJ and house music producer David Guetta featured Nicki singing and rapping on his song "Turn Me On" from his 2011 album *Nothing but the Beat*. The pair was the opening act for the 2011 American Music Awards in November 2011. They gave the audience a sneak peek at the song before its official release in January 2012. Accompanied by a high-tech video of mad scientist David creating automaton Nicki, the dance track hit No. 4 on the *Billboard* Top 100.

Nicki released the track "Starships" from *Roman Reloaded* on

Fighting words: Rapper Lil' Kim *(above)* and Nicki have feuded with each other through their songs. Here Lil' Kim sings at a Gay Pride event in Los Angeles in 2012.

Valentine's Day 2012. The first official release from the album, the song is upbeat and fun. With a spaceship and bikini-clad Nicki on the beaches in Hawaii, the video helped propel the song to the Top 10 in charts in Canada, western Europe, New Zealand, and Japan. Nicki was back!

The Eagle Has Landed
The full album dropped in regular and deluxe versions in April 2012. The regular version holds nineteen tracks, and the deluxe adds three more. (Typical albums average twelve

French connection: Nicki caught the attention of French DJ David Guetta, leading to their collaboration on his song "Turn Me On." The two *(above)* performed the song at the American Music Awards in 2011.

songs.) Catering to Nicki's wide fan base, the album is divided into hip-hop and dance-pop sections. It includes features by Lil Wayne, Chris Brown, and others and sold 253,000 copies in its first week.

After releasing "Starships," "Right by My Side,"and "Beez in the Trap" as singles, Nicki invited her fans to help her pick the next single from the album for release. Using Nicki's official website, MyPinkFriday .com, fans voted in May among songs, including "Marilyn Monroe," "Fire Burns," "Young Forever," "Pound the Alarm," "Whip It," and "Va Va Voom." With voter input and demand from radio listeners, "Pound the Alarm" became the winner.

Carnival Time

The techno-inspired dance song was a hit in nightclubs and reached No. 2 on the *Billboard* Hot Dance Club Songs and No. 15 on the *Billboard* Hot 100. It also became Nicki's third solo Top 10 hit in the United Kingdom. Nicki filmed a video for the song in Trinidad as a tribute to her beautiful home country. The video shows a number of picturesque locations around her hometown of Port of Spain. Nicki first wears a bra-and-panties outfit in the colors of the Trinidadian flag. She then appears in a red, feathered Carnival (pre-Easter festival) outfit and is joined by costumed festivalgoers for a street party. Stilt walkers, fire-breathers, confetti, and fireworks complete the fun. According to Nicki's Twitter feed, the four men in the final scene are her cousins.

While music videos show Nicki rapping and singing, she admits she's not much of a dancer. She says she interprets her words through dance and doesn't mind if people laugh with her or at her. She'd much rather be singing and rapping into her computer on GarageBand anyway.

Her First Solo Tour

To support her first album, Nicki had opened for Britney Spears and Lil Wayne. She was thrilled to announce her first headlining tour to support *Roman Reloaded*. After May dates in Australia and Japan, the Pink Friday tour moved on to Europe. The tour reunited Nicki with creative director and choreographer Laurieann Gibson, who had created her Grammy performance of *The Exorcism of Roman*. The show was typical Nicki Minaj, with multiple wig and costume changes and sets ranging from a church background, the interior of a spaceship, and Barbie's Dream House. Her outfits included a white tutu, a Marilyn Monroe-inspired dress, and graffiti leggings.

Nicki was also chosen to headline the flagship hip-hop concert Hot 97's Summer Jam. Held in New Jersey's MetLife Stadium, the concert was to include sets by a wide range of performers, including Waka Flocka Flame, Trey Songz, and 2 Chainz, among others. To be a female

Turned off: Nicki performing at the Hot 97 Summer Jam 2010, held in New Jersey. In 2012 she chose not to appear at the event after a dispute with the program's DJ.

MC and the headliner on a macho hip-hop stage was an unprecedented achievement.

The fifty-thousand people who packed the stadium on June 3, 2012, did not get to see Nicki, however. When Hot 97 DJ and *Hip Hop Squares* game-show host Peter Rosenberg introduced rapper Kendrick Lamar, he made a disparaging remark about Nicki's "Starships." He said it wasn't real hip-hop. Nicki felt disrespected and called Lil Wayne. Wayne immediately pulled her from the concert, as well as Cash Money acts DJ Khaled and Busta Rhymes. Wayne tweeted that Young Money was not going to participate in the event. Nicki tweeted that the organizers had messed up history. Nas and Lauryn Hill filled the empty headlining spot.

The Re-Up
Nicki's Pink Friday tour continued, with North American dates in July and August. The nineteen-city tour ended in New York City's Roseland

Over the moon: Nicki gleefully accepts the award for Best Female Video for "Starships" at the 2012 MTV Video Music Awards.

Ballroom on August 14. Not one to rest, Nicki announced a second set of international dates. Called the Pink Friday Reloaded tour, the fall concerts would be played in large arenas. Nicki promised they would be even bigger and crazier than the Pink Friday shows.

On the red carpet for the 2012 MTV Video Music Awards (VMAs) in September, Nicki had a surprise for her fans. Wearing a black lace bodysuit with red beaded detailing and built-in lighting, she told reporters she was rereleasing *Roman Reloaded*. The new album *Roman Reloaded—The Re-Up* would drop in November and include new material and new packaging. (Before that, the song "The Boys," featuring rapper Cassie, would be the first single to launch the album.) Later that evening, Nicki received a surprise of her own. She won the Moonman statuette for Best Female Video for "Starships."

Nicki earned another form of recognition a few weeks later. *Forbes* magazine released details of its top-earning hip-hop stars for the year. The only female on the list, Nicki was ranked No. 8. The Young Money team was well represented. Lil Wayne was No. 5 with earnings of $27 million, Drake was No. 6 with $20.5 million, Cash Money cofounder

Bryan "Birdman" Williams ranked seventh with $20 million, and Nicki was eighth with $15.5 million.

Idol Talk

Rumors that Nicki would be named an *American Idol* judge were confirmed in September 2012. Nicki joined judge Randy Jackson on a new panel with Mariah Carey and country singer Keith Urban. Gossip sites immediately began reporting

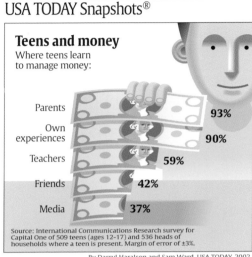

USA TODAY Snapshots®

Teens and money
Where teens learn
to manage money:

Parents	93%
Own experiences	90%
Teachers	59%
Friends	42%
Media	37%

Source: International Communications Research survey for
Capital One of 509 teens (ages 12-17) and 536 heads of
households where a teen is present. Margin of error of ±3%.

By Darryl Haralson and Sam Ward, USA TODAY, 2002

From the bench: Nicki joined Mariah Carey *(far left)* and Keith Urban *(second from left)* as a new judge on TV's *American Idol.* Along with the show's veteran judge Randy Jackson *(far right)*, the team announced the new lineup in New York in September 2012. Since then the media has been filled with gossip about the feuding between Nicki and Mariah.

New *American Idol* judges:
It's all about the girls

From the Pages of
USA TODAY

American Idol finally has set its judges' panel for Season 12—supreme diva Mariah Carey, rapper Nicki Minaj, country singer Keith Urban and sole holdover Randy Jackson. For fans who've kept abreast during the show's summer of speculation, there are no surprises here—except, possibly, for the retention of original judge Randy Jackson, who many had speculated would be relegated to a lower-profile mentoring role.

This overhaul could have a bigger impact on *Idol* than any other changes to the judges' table—more profound, even, than the departure of Simon Cowell after Season 9. It has the potential to rival the Season 7 decision to allow singers to start accompanying themselves on instruments, a rule change that coincided a five-year run of male Idols.

First, *Idol* producers are targeting a younger audience in a big way.... With its audience both aging and shrinking, *Idol* desperately needed to bring a fresh crop of younger viewers — and, more importantly, voters—to the show.

on tension between Mariah and Nicki. Nicki laughed off the talk of a feud, saying that Mariah was a legend she had always looked up to. The publicity was seen as good for the show, whose ratings had been dropping.

Another minor controversy erupted after Nicki seemed to endorse former Massachusetts governor Mitt Romney in the 2012 U.S. presidential election. On Lil Wayne's September 2012 mixtape, *Dedication 4*, Nicki raps that she's a Republican voting for Mitt

At 42, Carey's a pop-music icon, but she's no further past her prime than Jennifer Lopez was when she arrived on the *Idol* scene for Season 10 (besides, she's a year younger than Lopez). And *Idol* did wonders to resuscitate Lopez's music career. Minaj, 29, and Urban, 44, are both current hitmakers. They may not have Steven Tyler's appeal to the 50-somethings who've stuck with the show all these years, but they're a big deal in their formats.

The choice of new judges—particularly Minaj and Urban—suggest *Idol* producers know they need to appeal to certain genres. While bringing in Tyler didn't make *Idol* a viable launching pad for [budding] rock singers, country singers have always fared well on the show. Bringing in Urban, who proved himself to be a thoughtful mentor on the Australian edition of *The Voice*, can only increase interest in the show among country fans. The Trinidadian-born Minaj, on the other hand, addresses one of the show's weaknesses: its utter irrelevance to the contemporary R & B scene.

Most of all, though, the new judges' lineup augurs well for the next season's female contestants. Carey and Minaj—though surely unpredictable in many ways—can probably be counted on to nurture the young women, many of whom will have grown up idolizing and mimicking Carey. Urban, while he certainly commands respect from male country guitar players, appeals to a primarily female fan base.

With any luck, the additions of Carey, Minaj and Urban will renew the show's emphasis on female acts and change the voting audience just enough to produce a new type of *Idol*. Perhaps they'll bring in a new generation of young viewers, ones as willing to vote for a strong female singer as for a male heartthrob. Short of stacking the deck with a male roster full of Norman Gentles and Heejun Hans, the show's producers appear to have done all they can.

—Brian Mansfield

Romney. When reporters asked President Obama his thoughts about the rap, he replied that Nicki likes to play different characters and was perhaps joking. Nicki later tweeted to thank the president for understanding her sarcasm and creative humor. She signed off sending him love and support.

www.usatoday.com

USA TODAY
A GANNETT COMPANY

CHAPTER SEVEN

Girl power: Nicki *(center, with fans in New York)* shares a message of empowerment with her female fans. She feels passionately about women looking out for their own best interests.

Watch the Queen Conquer

A lot of Nicki's fierce girl-power appeal comes out of her traumatic childhood. Growing up with a verbally and physically abusive father and seeing her mother helpless to leave him gave Nicki an emotional toughness. She vowed never to be emotionally or financially dependent on a man. Looking back at her childhood, she sees that she mainly felt scared and trapped. That helplessness fueled her ferocious drive to succeed and to become rich. Nicki tells her female fans to have lives and careers separate from men. She also advises them to stay celibate, to stay in school, and to stay focused on their career goals rather than on boys. She describes her ideal man as old, wrinkled, and white, on a green piece of paper.

Nicki's biggest sense of accomplishment comes from providing for her mother. She says she's most proud of buying her mom a home in Carol's own name. "I got her the house I always wanted to live in when I was a kid," she recalls. "I finally could breathe this sigh of relief. No one could ever really understand because people equate different types of goals with that moment when you feel really accomplished. Like people think, Oh well, you broke *Billboard* records or, You signed with Lil Wayne. But to me, the one thing that I had been driving toward was buying my mom a home."

Nicki has always been outspoken about wanting to build a global business. Even in August 2009 (well before *Pink Friday* was released), Nicki spoke candidly about being a businesswoman first and a rapper second. In an interview with VladTV.com, Nicki explained her point of view. "You can't come into this business thinking it's all about music, this is a business. In any business, whatever you're marketing, whatever you're selling, you have to do your homework on the market. . . . I wanted to explore the business and take it to where the guys take it as a businesswoman. So my music is only one facet of the empire I'm building."

She went on to explain that she's not a female rapper, she's an entertainer. Nicki knew early on that success means branding. So she has been intent on carefully constructing the Nicki Minaj brand. For example, even though her wardrobe changes frequently, she's instantly recognizable by her long eyelashes and by her wigs inspired by Japanese anime (animation). The combination has become like a Nicki Minaj logo.

USA TODAY
Life
SECTION D
LIFE.USATODAY.COM

November 23, 2010

Nicki Minaj Brings Her Theatrical Style to *Pink Friday* [Excerpt 4]

<u>From the Pages of</u>
<u>USA TODAY</u>

Taking charge has, by all appearances, come naturally to Minaj, whom Lil Wayne discovered and signed to his Young Money label in 2008. Though *Pink Friday* is her first album, she is already known for her sassy featured spots on numerous hit singles by top stars, among them Wayne's "Knockout," Usher's "Lil Freak," Trey Songz's "Bottoms Up" and Kanye West's "Monster" (with Jay-Z).

For *Pink Friday*, Minaj recruited an equally impressive guest list. Various tracks find her sharing the mike with West, Eminem, Rihanna, will.i.am, Drake and Natasha Bedingfield. "Have you ever seen an album this star-studded—from a girl?" Minaj asks, with characteristic forthrightness.

Broad appeal

Minaj's gender makes her meteoric rise in the rap world an even bigger story. "Your Love," *Pink Friday*'s Annie Lennox-sampling first single, recently became the first track by a female solo artist to top the *Billboard* rap chart. Minaj has cited women as diverse as Lauryn Hill, Missy Elliott and Bedingfield as influences on her strong but sensual and decidedly quirky voice, which incorporates various personae she describes as alter egos.

"In a really short time, she has established herself as the premier female rapper right now, and maybe one of the top three of all time," says *Rolling Stone* senior editor Michael Endelman. "And she's managed to appeal to a wide range of fans, from younger teenage girls to pop connoisseurs who see her as a real talent with a unique point of view."

Minaj likes to call her music "hip-*pop*. I'm an MC, I'm a lyricist, and I put my all into delivering the best rap line ever. But I also feel the need to hit all angles of pop culture. What I do is hip-hop meets top 40 meets theater." And like Gaga, Minaj manifests those influences and aspirations visually as well as musically.

—Elysa Gardner

Mass appeal: Nicki has made a point to perform with a range of musical talent, including R & B's Usher *(left)* and pop's Cassie *(right)*. As a result, she appeals to a wide range of music lovers.

Rule the World

Nicki has smartly associated herself with existing brands to give her own brand instant credibility and cool factor. For example, appearing on twenty other artist's songs in 2010 allowed Nicki to increase her popularity. And appearing with artists as different as Christina Aguilera, Ludacris, and Usher helped her expand her fan beyond hip-hop to R & B and pop. It also helped get her widely played on radio.

In addition, Nicki was savvy in building her social media base. She didn't just passively allow fans to come on board as Twitter followers or Facebook fans. She engaged directly with them. She answers questions often and retweets posts, cultivating fans to become passionate about all things Nicki.

Before her first album came out, Nicki and executives from Young Money met with John Demsey, president of MAC Cosmetics. Nicki was direct. She wanted to be the 2011 face of Viva Glam, a line of MAC lipsticks and lip glosses that raise money for people affected by HIV/AIDS. Demsey was impressed with Nicki's style, but she wasn't yet as

USA TODAY Snapshots®

Makeup women wear daily

Percentage of women who say:

Mascara and/or eyeliner	78%
Foundation and/or concealer	66%
Blush and/or bronzer	56%
Lipstick and/or lip gloss	54%

Source: Self magazine survey of 2,000 readers

By Michelle Healy and Veronica Bravo, USA TODAY, 2011

Lip color: Nicki and MAC Cosmetics launched the Pink Friday lipstick right after the release of Nicki's *Pink Friday* album in 2010.

big a star as Lady Gaga or Fergie, who had also represented the brand.

Demsey suggested that they launch a special Pink Friday lipstick to go on sale on the four Fridays after the album's November 2010 release. The three thousand lipsticks in stock sold out in fifteen minutes that first Friday, followed by a staggering twenty-seven thousand in the next three weeks. Most of the sales came from Nicki's millions of Twitter and Facebook followers. When Nicki tweeted that the *Pink Friday* album was available for preorder on Amazon, her Barbz retweeted and reposted the news, helping the album move from 500th place to No. 4 in minutes. Demsey was happy to nurture Nicki's fans and continue the MAC relationship. He cast her alongside Ricky Martin as the 2012 face of Viva Glam.

The Power of the Law

Nicki works incredibly hard. She's normally in the studio by nine or ten in the morning, keeping business hours. Unless she has a concert, she doesn't stay out late. She's usually in bed by nine or ten at night. She keeps her energy up during the day by snacking on almonds and cranberries between meals. Another key to her success has been good representation. Nicki credits hip-hop and R & B record producer Irv Gotti, founder of The Inc record label, with hooking her up with good lawyers early in her career. He promised the legal team that while Nicki couldn't afford to pay them right away, if they stuck with her, she would pay them well later. The lawyers, who signed on before Nicki's debut album, were responsible for getting her a great 360 deal with Cash Money/Young Money.

Nicki's legal team, combined with management company Blueprint

Recession fuels shift from

IN F⊕CUS

360 Deal

A 360 deal refers to the contract between an artist and a record label. The label agrees to provide financial support for the artist up front, including cash advances as well as funds for marketing, promotion, and touring. In return, the artist gives the company a percentage of all of his or her income, from sales of recorded music, tours and performances, and any other income. It means that the record company outlays a huge amount of money in the beginning, with great risk if the artist isn't successful. A 360 deal usually goes to artists who are "safe," with a proven track record, such as Madonna and Jay-Z. For someone without a record, a deal like this is almost unheard of. Acknowledging the role of her legal team in her success, Nicki gave the team a shout out in her feature on Drake's "Make Me Proud."

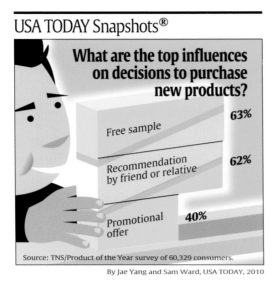

USA TODAY Snapshots®

What are the top influences on decisions to purchase new products?

Free sample **63%**

Recommendation by friend or relative **62%**

Promotional offer **40%**

Source: TNS/Product of the Year survey of 60,329 consumers.

By Jae Yang and Sam Ward, USA TODAY, 2010

Group, has helped her ink deals in various industries. With her 21 million Facebook fans and 14 million Twitter followers, Nicki brings with her a built-in young audience, eager to buy a piece of celebrity. Lots of brands would like a piece of that action. Nicki teamed up with OPI Nail Lacquer with a limited edition collection of *Pink Friday*-themed colors, including Super Bass Shatter and Metallic 4 Life. Adidas designer Jeremy Scott signed Nicki as the face of the Fall 2012 collection for Adidas. The collection borrows some of her Japanese-influenced style for the bubble-gum colors of the clothing and shoes.

"In This Very Moment I'm King"

Nicki's most lucrative deal so far is a multimillion-dollar contract with Pepsi. In addition to an ad campaign for the cola, Nicki will be the face of a soda called Pop. With ads filmed in secret, Pepsi is counting on Nicki's quirky, fun, and exciting personality to jazz up the Pop brand. The agreement works both ways. It brings the soda to Nicki's fans and exposes Nicki to all corners of the globe. "Nicki has momentum. She's a maverick," says Frank Cooper of PepsiCo. "We want to help her . . . gain momentum in territories outside the U.S., and build in China where she doesn't have as much of a presence as she does here."

Plans are also afoot for a Nicki Minaj clothing line. Nicki says, "The clothing line is coming out very, very amazing and pretty . . . but I'm not rushing that one. . . . It has to be amazing and really, really specific to Barbz, ya know what I mean?" Nicki says the designers are working on sketches inspired by outfits she's worn and by looks she loves. Her Barbz are also eating up her smartphone and My Pink Friday iPad app. The app features the Nictionary—a list of Nicki's vocabulary read by Nicki herself—as well as photo galleries, song samples, news, and upcoming events. It also offers ways to interact on Facebook and Twitter. Even businesses without

Cola campaign: As part of her drive to be a successful businesswoman, Nicki agreed to promote Pepsi. The image above shows her on the set of one of the Pepsi commercials.

direct agreements with Nicki are seeing an uptick in sales. Wigs in multiple colors and thick bangs are selling like crazy. Nicki Minaj costumes are a huge seller for Halloween.

Feeling Charitable

Nicki's not just all about the money though. She signed a licensing agreement with Give Back Brands to create a Nicki Minaj signature scent. Give Back Brands partners with celebrities to create products that give some of the money from sales to charities of the artist's choice. The perfume bottle features a long pink wig atop a replica of Nicki's face and chest. She declared, "I designed this scent and bottle with my Barbz in mind; I know they will love it!"

Eau de parfum: Nicki holds her fruit-scented Pink Friday perfume, which launched in the fall of 2012. The perfume comes in a Nicki look-alike bottle.

Nicki was thrilled when Mattel created a one-of-a-kind Nicki Minaj Barbie doll for auction at Charitybuzz.com. She was surprised when they chose her for the doll, and incredibly proud. For Mattel it was a no-brainer. Barbie is a pop culture icon, and Nicki is a pop and fashion icon—and a big Barbie fan. Bids for the doll started at $1,000 and closed at almost $15,000. Proceeds went to Project Angel Food, a meal service for people with HIV/AIDS.

The Price of Fame

Nicki admits there can be a downside to her enormous popularity and fame. "I'm already a shy person," she told ABC's Juju Chang on *Nightline*. "I don't really like crowds, really. Sometimes I want to just pull the off switch, but you can't because if you go outside, you have to give people your all. You can't say, 'Oh, you know what? I'm not feeling good today.' No. No one's trying to hear that. When a woman comes up to you and says, 'Hey, my daughter's your biggest fan. Can we have a picture?' You can't say no."

On tour in England, Nicki attracted so many fans that the hotel management requested that she leave by the back entrance. Nicki couldn't bear to. She felt she would be letting the fans down after they'd waited so patiently for a glimpse of her. Instead, she changed hotels.

She says that her life is stressful but that she wouldn't change it for the world. Sometimes she'd like to get a few hours more sleep or just relax. But she knows that in the entertainment business, you've got to

IN FCUS

Nictionary

These are some of the terms from Nicki's Nictionary, an app for smartphones that features Nicki reading definitions of her phrases:

Barbie boom box: a device that plays Barbie's fetch music

chuckles: when a Barbie laughs at the expense of one of her friends

copyrightin' infringements: girls who claim to be rappers while enlisting the help of ghostwriters

dollhouse: a place where Barbie stays while away on business

Dolly Lama: a Barbie who makes everyone around her feel at peace; a problem solver; the one you call when you're at you're worst

fetch: a term to describe something a Barbie really likes

get off my fone: a swift dismissal of a stupid phone call or comment

HB: abbreviation of Harajuku Barbie, one of Nicki's alter egos. Harajuku refers to a fashionable area and shopping district in Tokyo, Japan.

constantly be fresh and in front of the public. She likes being able to provide for her mom and put her nieces through college. She enjoys not having to worry about money and being independent.

Still, she's conscious that no matter what she does, her fans want more. The expectation is always to go higher and higher. She tries to remain grounded and give as much as she can without losing herself. She says she'd much rather give more than regret not giving enough. However, sometimes she feels as if she's lost her peace of mind, no longer knowing who is a friend and who is an enemy. She says she's always wondering if people are calling her because they like her or because they want a photo of her. She has to remind herself that she's only been a big star for a few years. She remembers—this is only the beginning.

USA TODAY

Life

SECTION D

LIFE.USATODAY.COM

March 22, 2012

Small Business Strategies: Women get into the startup game

<u>From the Pages of</u>
<u>USA TODAY</u>

I don't normally go gaga over motorcycles, but even I couldn't resist the shiny new scooter from Current Motor. . . .

Perhaps one of the most surprising aspects of this cutting-edge product is that this company has a woman president, is financed by women investors, and is made in a manufacturing plant owned by a woman.

Why surprising? Here's a sad truth in 2012: Women entrepreneurs still have a harder time raising money for high-growth ventures than men.

That situation is changing, thanks to women like Lauren Flanagan of Belle Capital of Grosse Pointe Farms, Mich. Flanagan represents a relatively new breed of angel investors, experienced businesswomen investing in startups founded by women.

"Women have over 51 percent of the wealth in the U.S., but we do less than 10 percent of early stage investing," Flanagan said. "We have women with talent and money sitting on the sideline.

"If we could get some of that money invested, we'd change the game," she said. "We could break the cycle of lack of access to capital for women entrepreneurs."

To understand financing for high-growth companies, it helps to understand the two types of professional investors and lack of women in these ranks:

•Venture capitalists raise money from others, typically investing very large sums of money—$2 million to $5 million and more in early rounds. About 11 percent of venture capitalists are women, according to the National Venture Capital Association, and estimates are that only 4 percent to 9 percent of companies receiving venture-capital financing have even one woman on the founding team.

•Angel investors put their own money into promising startups. About 13 percent of angels are women, and about 13 percent of angel-backed companies have women founders.

Keep in mind that nearly half of all businesses in the United States have a female owner: 29 percent owned by women alone, 17 percent equally owned with a man. So you see what a small percentage have access to high-growth capital.

Increasingly, women are starting their own angel-investor groups to make it easier for women entrepreneurs with great ideas to succeed. . . .

Flanagan herself has invested in about 30 companies. In 2005, she launched her first group, Phenomenelle Angels Fund in Madison, Wis.

That group invested about $10 million and raised another $30 million for nine companies, all of which have a woman founder or significant C-level partner, a term used to denote high-ranking executives such as chief executive officers, chief operating officers and chief investment officers.

All the investors are women, and they project hitting their target on financial gains.

Last year, she started Belle Capital with 44 women investors. One of its first investments is Current Motor Co. of Ann Arbor, Mich., makers of that shiny, new electric scooter.

Belle Capital has brought far more than money to this promising startup.

"We leverage our financial capital with our human capital," Flanagan said. "One of our partners is Andra Rush, she's the founder of two companies that combined have over a billion dollars of revenue. . . ."

Belle Capital, www.bellevc.com, and Flanagan are part of a nationwide movement to increase women's access to venture financing. Other places to check:

• Astia, www.astia.org
• Golden Seeds, www.goldenseeds.com
• Springboard Enterprises, www.springboardenterprises.org
• Women 2.0, www.women2.org
• Women's Capital Connection of Kansas City, www.onekcforwomen.com

And soon, look for a Current Motor electric scooter on a street near you.

—Rhonda Abrams

What's Next?

Nicki is an eager learner and a strong-minded businessperson. She's learned from successful moguls such as Jay-Z. She feels that if they can do it, she can too. She says that being a girl makes no difference. She's determined to dominate multiple areas of business.

Nicki has her own record label, Pink Friday Productions, and is free to sign people who appeal to her. So far she has signed several producers but no musical artists. Nicki worries that if she signed an artist now, she wouldn't have the time to dedicate to that person's career. She knows how it feels to depend on someone else for your big break. She doesn't want to hold someone's dreams in her hand and let anyone down.

Nicki's home life is more settled, as she continues to repair her strained relationship with her father. She says that Robert went to rehab years ago and got sober. He began joining Carol at church and started changing his life. They even had a third child together, Nicki's little brother Makiya. Nicki says her father doesn't instill fear in anyone anymore, but she hasn't completely let her guard down. She says she's vowed never to let anyone control her or be an alcoholic around her because she never wants any children of hers to go through what she did. She has defined one of her goals to be life without struggle.

Nicki's financial success has allowed her mother to stop working so hard. Inspired by her daughter's strength and by her own deep religious faith, Carol now shares her experiences with others. She gives motivational speeches at the Center Against Domestic Violence in Manhattan. She also hopes to work with battered women in Trinidad and Tobago. With the support from older women at her church, she is writing an inspirational book and would like to release a gospel single. She forgives Robert. She says he was beaten often as a child, which contributed to why he became an abuser as an adult man.

At this point in Nicki's career, she doesn't have a lot of hobbies or downtime. Her idea of fun is staying home and watching *Judge Judy* or *Curb Your Enthusiasm*. She says she cooks a mean boneless chicken stew but complains she never has any time to cook. She plans to write books, including one featuring Roman, and she wants to be on TV and in movies. Toward this goal, she is scheduled for a trilogy of reality specials on the E! Channel. Nicki has also told interviewers that she'd love to get married and have a baby. But she's very clear that it would not occur anytime soon. She wants to win a Grammy and an Oscar first.

Nicki takes her position as a role model very seriously. She wants to show girls that they can succeed in any business if they apply themselves. "I want to show little girls that the possibilities are endless. That's my goal—to not only do it for myself, but to show them I can do whatever I put my mind to."

On the other hand, Nicki has her beloved mom to keep her grounded in reality. She says her mom couldn't tell the difference between Alicia Keys and Beyoncé and would rather talk about her problems with a plumber than hear about the latest crazy thing Nicki has planned. One thing's for certain. Whether in her role as Roman Zolanski, Barbie, a lauded celebrity, or a faithful daughter, Nicki Minaj will continue to reconfigure, redefine, and conquer hip-hop and pop culture for some time to come.

On top of her game: Nicki's business smarts, hard work, and commitment to her career have made her a powerful force in the world of entertainment.

TRACK LISTS

Pink Friday (2010)

1. "I'm the Best"
2. "Roman's Revenge" (Feat. Eminem)
3. "Did It On 'Em"
4. "Right Thru Me"
5. "Fly" (Feat. Rihanna)
6. "Save Me"
7. "Moment 4 Life" (Feat. Drake)
8. "Check It Out" (with will.i.am)
9. "Blazin'" (Feat. Kanye West)
10. "Here I Am"
11. "Dear Old Nicki"
12. "Your Love"
13. "Last Chance" (Feat. Natasha Bedingfield)

Deluxe Edition Bonus Tracks

14. "Super Bass"
15. "Blow Ya Mind"
16. "Muny"

Pink Friday: Roman Reloaded (2012)

1. "Roman Holiday"
2. "Come on a Cone"
3. "I Am Your Leader" (Feat. Cam'ron and Rick Ross)
4. "Beez in the Trap" (Feat. 2 Chainz)
5. " HOV Lane"
6. "Roman Reloaded" (Feat. Lil Wayne)
7. "Champion" (Feat. Nas, Drake, and Young Jeezy)
8. "Right by My Side" (Feat. Chris Brown)
9. "Sex in the Lounge" (Feat. Lil Wayne and Bobby V)
10. "Starships"

11. "Pound the Alarm"
12. "Whip It"
13. "Automatic"
14. "Beautiful Sinner"
15. "Marilyn Monroe"
16. "Young Forever"
17. "Fire Burns"
18. "Gun Shot" (Feat. Beenie Man)
19. "Stupid H—"

Deluxe Edition Bonus Tracks
20. "Turn Me On"
21. "Va Va Voom"
22. "Masquerade"

AWARDS AND NOMINATIONS

American Music Awards
2011
> Won
> Category: Favorite Rap/Hip-Hop Artist

2011
> Won
> Category: Favorite Rap/Hip-Hop Album for *Pink Friday*

BET Awards
2012
> Won
> Category: Best Female Hip-Hop Artist

2011
> Won
> Category: Best Female Hip-Hop Artist

2011
> Nominated
> Category: Viewers' Choice Award for "Moment 4 Life" (shared with Drake)

2010
> Won
> Category: Best Female Hip-Hop Artist

2010
> Won
> Category: Best New Artist

BET Hip-Hop Awards
2012
> Nominated
> Category: Made-You-Look (Best Hip-Hop Style)

2011
> Won
> Category: Made-You-Look Award (Best Hip-Hop Style)

2011
Won
Category: MVP of the Year

2011
Nominated
Category: Sweet 16: Best Featured Verse for "Monster" (shared with Kanye West, Jay-Z, Rick Ross, and Bon Iver)

2011
Nominated
Category: CD of the Year for *Pink Friday*

2011
Nominated
Category: Verizon People's Champ Award (Viewers' Choice) for "Moment 4 Life" (shared with Drake)

2011
Nominated
Category: Lyricist of the Year

2010
Won
People's Champ Award

2010
Won
Category: Rookie of the Year

2010
Won Made-You-Look Award

2010
Nominated
Category: Hustler of the Year

Billboard Music Awards
2012
Won
Category: Top Streaming Song (Video) for "Super Bass"

2012
Nominated
Category: Top Female Artist

2012
> Nominated
> Category: Top Radio Songs Artist

2012
> Nominated
> Category: Top Streaming Artist

2012
> Nominated
> Category: Top Rap Artist

2012
> Nominated
> Category: Top Streaming Song (Audio) for "Super Bass"

2012
> Nominated
> Category: Top Rap Song for "Super Bass"

2011
> Nominated
> Category: Top Rap Artist

2011
> Nominated
> Category: Top Rap Album for *Pink Friday*

2011
> Nominated
> Category: Top New Artist

Brit Awards

2012
> Nominated
> Category: International Breakthrough Act

Grammy Awards

2012
> Nominated
> Category: Best New Artist

2012

Nominated

Category: Best Rap Album for *Pink Friday*

2012

Nominated

Category: Best Rap Performance for "Moment 4 Life" (shared with Drake)

2011

Nominated

Category: Best Rap Performance by a Duo or Group for "My Chick Bad" (shared with Ludacris)

MOBO (Music of Black Origin) Awards (United Kingdom)

2011

Nominated

Category: Best International Act

2010

Nominated

Category: Best International Act

MTV Video Music Awards

2012

Won

Category: Best Female Video

2012

Nominated

Category: Best Hip-Hop Video for "Beez in the Trap" (featuring 2 Chainz)

2012

Nominated

Category: Best Visual Effects for "Turn Me On" (Nicki Minaj and David Guetta)

2011

Won

Category: Best Hip-Hop Video for "Super Bass"

2011
    Nominated
    Category: Best Collaboration for "Moment 4 Life" (shared with Drake)
2011
    Nominated
    Category: Best Female Video for "Super Bass"
2010
    Nominated
    Category: Best New Artist for "Massive Attack" (shared with Sean
    Garrett)

Much Music Video Awards (Canada)
2012
    Nominated
    Category: International Video of the Year—Artist for "Starships"

NAACP Image Awards
2011
    Nominated
    Category: Outstanding New Artist

O Music Awards
2012
    Won
    Category: Too Much A— for TV
2012
    Nominated
    Category: Most Intense Social Splat
2011
    Won
    Category: Favorite Animated GIF
2011
    Nominated
    Category: Must-Follow Artist on Twitter

People's Choice Awards, USA
2012
>Nominated
>Category: Favorite Hip-Hop Artist

Soul Train Music Awards
2011
>Won
>Category: Best Hip-Hop Song of the Year for "Moment 4 Life"

2010
>Nominated
>Category: Best New Artist

2010
>Nominated
>Category: Best Hip-Hop Song of the Year for "Your Love"

Teen Choice Awards
2012
>Won
>Category: Choice R&B/Hip-Hop Song for "Starships"

2012
>Nominated
>Category: Choice Fashion Icon: Female

2012
>Won
>Category: Choice R & B/Hip-Hop Artist

2011
>Nominated
>Category: Choice Music: R & B/Hip-Hop Artist

2011
>Nominated
>Category: Choice Summer Song for "Super Bass"

SOURCE NOTES

6. MTV, "Nicki Minaj: My Time Now," *MTV.com*, November 28, 2010, http://www.mtv.com/shows/nicki_minaj_my_time_now/series.jhtml (May 30, 2012).

7. E! Entertainment, "E Special: Nicki Minaj," *eonline.com*, July 12, 2011, http://www.eonline.com/videos/E__Special__Nicki_Minaj/167166 (May 30, 2012).

21. God-Meta, "Always Been a Businessman: Interview with Hip-Hop Mogul Fendi "Da Mayor," *NCHipHopConnect.com,* October 6, 2010, http://www.nchiphopconnect.com/fendi10510.php (April 17, 2012).

21. Ibid.

22. Ibid.

24. E Entertainment, "E Special: Nicki Minaj."

30. Jayson Rodriguez, "Nicki Minaj Shocked By #1 Hit 'Your Love,'" *MTV News,* July 6, 2010, http://www.mtv.com/videos/news/535146/nicki-minaj-talks-being-the-first-female-rapper-to-have-a-1-song-in-over-eight-years.jhtml (April 17, 2012).

31–32. Angie Martinez, "Kanye West Calls Nicki Minaj the #2 Rapper of All Time," *Hot97.com*, August 11, 2010, http://www.youtube.com/watch?v=F19feUizUeQ (May 30, 2012).

32–33. Rap-Up TV, "Rick Ross Says 'Monster' Made Him a Nicki Minaj Believer," *Rap-Up.com*, September 16, 2010, http://www.rap-up.com/2010/09/16/rap-up-tv-rick-ross-says-monster-made-him-a-nicki-minaj-believer/ (April 18, 2012).

42. Andrea Lavinthal, "Nicki Minaj Suffered 'Horrible' Wardrobe Malfunction," *Us Weekly*, March 21, 2012, http://www.usmagazine.com/celebrity-style/news/nicki-minaj-suffered-horrible-wardrobe-malfunction-2012213 (October 4, 2012).

45. Complex Media, "Nicki Minaj: Self Possessed," *Complex*, March 20, 2012, http://www.complex.com/music/2012/03/nicki-minaj-cover-story (April 22, 2012).

49. Ibid.

50. Manny Norte, "UK Radio Interview: Nicki Minaj," *KISS FM UK*, January 23, 2011, http://youtube.com/watch?v=/Xv8kPBqbc5M (April 18, 2012).

51. Nick Haramis, "The Meteoric Rise of Nicki Minaj," *Black Book*,

February 23, 2011, http://www.blackbookmag.com/music/the-meteoric-rise-of-nicki-minaj-1.37639 (April 15, 2012).

56. Ibid.

58–59. T. Cole Rachel, "Nicki Minaj on Lil Wayne," *Interview*, March 28, 2011, http://www.interviewmagazine.com/music/nicki-minaj-on-lil-wayne/#_ (April 22, 2012).

59. Judith Newman, "Just Try to Look Away," *Allure*, April 2012, 236.

60. *Teen Vogue*, "Ten Questions for Nicki Minaj," April 2011, http://www.teenvogue.com/style/2011/04/nicki-minaj-interview#slide=1 (April 22, 2010).

61. Ibid.

61. Ibid.

62. Chuck Arnold and Jessica Herndon, "Nicki Minaj's Top 5 Style Idols," *People*, December 6, 2010, http://www.people.com/people/archive/article/0,,20445758,00.html (April 22, 2010).

70. Complex Media, "Nicki Minaj: Self Possessed."

71. Ibid.

72–73. Michael Murray, "World Premiere: Listen to Nicki Minaj's New Single 'Starships,'" February 14, 2012, http://ryanseacrest.com/2012/02/14/world-premiere-listen-to-nicki-minajs-new-single-starships-audio (May 25, 2012).

73. Ibid.

83. Newman, "Just Try to Look Away," 238.

83. DJ Vlad, "Exclusive: Nicki Minaj Talks Female Rappers," *Vladtv.com*, August 23, 2009, http://www.youtube.com/watch?v=nPA7j2RKHII&playnext=1&list=PL6C6FDB063DEBAFB2 (May 7, 2012).

88. Andrew Hampp, "The Cola Wars: How Pepsi and Coke Are Battling in the Music Space," *Billboard.biz*, April 30, 2012, http://www.billboard.biz/bbbiz/industry/branding/the-cola-wars-how-pepsi-and-coke-are-battling-1006904552.story (May 2, 2012).

88–89. Tim Westwood, "Nicki Minaj New Perfume, Clothing Line, Working with Pepsi " *Westwoodtv.com*, April 25, 2012, http://www.youtube.com/watch?v=ebOywnbRBf4&feature=player_embedded (May 7, 2012).

89. Nicki Minaj, "Give Back Brands Signs Exclusive Fragrance," *MyPinkFriday*, April 23, 2012, http://mypinkfriday.com/news/73601 (May 2, 2012).

90. JuJu Chang, "The Minaj Effect," *Nightline*, April 9, 2012, http://abcnews.go.com/Nightline/video/nicki-minaj-pop-singer-music-16105666 (May 25, 2012).

95. Simon Hattenstone, "Nicki Minaj: 'I Have Bigger Balls Than the Boys.'" *Guardian* (London), April 27, 2012, http://m.guardian.co.uk/ms/p/gnm/op/view.m?id=15&gid=/music/2012/apr/27/nicki-minaj-bigger-balls-than-the-boys&cat=music (October 4, 2012).

SELECTED BIBLIOGRAPHY

AceShowbiz Staff. "Nicki Minaj Awards." *AceShowbiz.com*. N.d. http://www. aceshowbiz.com/celebrity/nicki_minaj/awards.html (May 25, 2012).

Cummings, Renee. "Carol Maraj—Mother of Hip Hop Star Nicki Minaj." *Trinidad Express*, July 21, 2012. http://www.trinidadexpress.com/ woman-magazine/Carol_Maraj-163265826.html (September 30, 2012).

Desrosiers, Kendra. "4 Reasons Why Rapper Nicki Minaj Should Manage Your Brand." *Hubspot* (blog). July 6, 2011. http://blog.hubspot.com/blog /tabid/6307/bid/18641/4-Reasons-Why-Rapper-Nicki-Minaj-Should-Manage-Your-Brand.aspx (May 25, 2012).

Dodes, Rachel. "Madonna Watches the Throne." *Wall Street Journal*, January 27, 2012. http://blogs.wsj.com/speakeasy/2012/01/27/madonna-watches-the-throne/ (May 1, 2012).

DX Staff. "The 2010 HipHopDX Year End Awards." *HipHopDX*. December 13, 2010. http://www.hiphopdx.com/index/editorials/id.1633 /title.the-2010-hiphopdx-year-end-awards (April 18, 2012).

Holson, Laura M. "It's Nicki's World." *New York Times Style Magazine*. January 7, 2012. http://www.nytimes.com/2012/01/08/fashion/nicki-minaj-as-a-rising-style-muse.html (April 10, 2012).

Iandoli, Kathy. "Nicki Minaj Makes History with Seven *Billboard* Hot 100 Songs." *MTV News*, October, 8, 2010. http://rapfix.mtv.com/2010/10/08 /nicki-minaj-makes-history-with-seven-billboard-hot-100-songs/ (April 18, 2012).

Rodriguez, Jayson, with reporting by Matt Elias. "Nicki Minaj 'Manifested' Rihanna for 'Fly' Feature." *mtv.com*. November 30, 2010. http://www. mtv.com/news/articles/1653259/nicki-minaj-manifested-rihanna-fly-feature-jr-rotem.jhtml (April 23, 2012).

Sullivan, Kate. "Nicki Minaj's Hairstylist Terrence Davidson Talks Wigs." *Allure.com*. October 6, 2011. http://www.allure.com/beauty-trends /blogs/daily-beauty-reporter/2011/10/nicki-minajs-hairstylist-terre.html (April 22, 2012).

U.S. Department of Justice. "DEA History Book, 1876–1990." N.d., *Justice. gov*. http://www.justice.gov/dea/pubs/history/1985–1990.html (April 23, 2012).

U.S. Department of State. "Background Note: Trinidad and Tobago." *State. Gov.* December 16, 2011. http://www.state.gov/r/pa/ei/bgn/35638.htm (April 23, 2012).

FURTHER READING AND WEBSITES

Books

Abarbanel, Karin. *Birthing the Elephant: The Woman's Go-for-It! Guide to Overcoming the Big Challenges of Launching a Business*. Berkley, CA: Ten Speed Press, 2008.

Boyd, Christie Brewer. *Nicki Minaj*. Farmington Hills, MI: Lucent Books, 2013.

Doeden, Matt. *Lady Gaga: Pop's Glam Queen*. Minneapolis: Twenty-First Century Books, 2012.

Golus, Carrie. *Tupac Shakur: Hip-Hop Idol*. Minneapolis: Twenty-First Century Books, 2010.

Holloway, Lynette. *Nicki Minaj: The Woman Who Stole the World*. Phoenix: Amber Books, 2012.

Kaplan, Arie. *American Pop: Hit Makers, Superstars, and Dance Revolutionaries*. Minneapolis: Twenty-First Century Books, 2013.

Morgan, Kayla. *Kanye West: Soul-Fired Hip-Hop*. Minneapolis: Twenty-First Century Books, 2012.

Sacks, Nathan. *American Hip-Hop: Rappers, DJs, and Hard Beats*. Minneapolis: Twenty-First Century Books, 2013.

Websites

Billboard
http://www.Billboard.com
The music industry's official chart-tracking organization features artist biographies, chart history for songs and albums, track-by-track album reviews, news, and discussion.

HipHopDX
http://www.HipHopDX.com
This hip-hop site tracks breaking news, songs, video, and mixtapes, plus interviews, album reviews, and editorials.

My Pink Friday
: http://www.MyPinkFriday.com
  Nicki's official website lists news, concerts, and other events, as well as her blog, a live fan twitter feed, and community forum.

Nicki Minaj/Facebook
: http://www.Facebook.com/nickiminaj
  Nicki's official Facebook page has news, photos, and contests for fans.

Rolling Stone
: www.RollingStone.com
  Rolling Stone magazine's website contains music news, song and album reviews, artist videos, photos, playlists, and more.

INDEX

PHOTO ACKNOWLEDGEMENTS

The images in this book are used with the permission of: © Kevin Winter/DCNYRE2012/Getty Images for DCP, p. 1; © Steve Granitz/WireImage/Getty Images, p. 3; © Angela Boatwright/Retna Ltd., p. 4; www.myspace.com/nickiminaj, p. 5; © Paul Thompson/Photolibrary/Getty Images, p. 6; © Bertrand Guay/AFP/Getty Images, p. 8; © Lee Snider/Dreamstime.com, p. 9; © Tim Loehrke/USA TODAY, p. 10; © Jym Wilson/USA TODAY, p. 11; © D. Dipasupil/FilmMagic/Getty Images, pp. 13, 20, 29, 32 (top), 36, 38, 46 (top), 54, 60 (top), 68 (top), 70, 80, 84, 92; © Ellen McKnight/Alamy, p. 14; © Bryan Bedder/Getty Images, p. 16 (top); © Jason Merritt/ Getty Images, p. 18; © Ray Tamarra/Getty Images, p. 19; © Timothy Hiatt/Stringer/Getty Images p. 21; © Ben Rose/Picture Group via AP Images, p. 23; © Jared Milgrim/FilmMagic/Getty Images. p. 25; © Neilson Barnard/Stringer/Getty Images, p. 28; © Johnny Nunez/WireImage/Getty Images, p. 30; © Kevin Mazur/WireImage/Getty Images, pp. 31, 48; © Paul Abell/PictureGroup via AP Images, p. 32 (bottom); USA TODAY, p. 34, 56(right); Matt Baron/BEImages/Rex USA, p. 35; © Dana Edelson/NBC/NBCU Photo Bank via Getty Images, p. 37; Lucy Nicholson/Reuters/ Landov, p. 39; © Dan MacMedan/USA TODAY, pp. 41, 46 (bottom), 56 (left), 60 (bottom); © H. Darr Beiser/USA TODAY, p. 44; © Robert Hanashiro/USA TODAY, p. 47; AP Photo/Jonathan Short , p. 49; Beretta/Sims/Rex/Rex USA, p. 51; © Ethan Miller/Getty Images for ACB, p. 52; NC1 WENN Photos/Newscom, p. 53; © Walik Goshorn/Retna Ltd./CORBIS, pp. 55, 82; © Christopher Polk/Getty Images for Clear Channel, p. 58; © Terry Lott/Sony Music Archive/Getty Images, p. 59; © Debra L. Rothenberg/FilmMagic/Getty Images, p. 61; © Denise Truscello/WireImage/ Getty Images, p. 62; Russ Elliot/AdMedia/Newscom, p. 63; © Frank Trapper/CORBIS, p. 64 (top); © Mike Copploa/Getty Images for Mercedes-Benz Fashion Week, p. 64 (bottom); © Emmanuel Faure/The Image Bank/Getty Images, p. 66; © Neil Mockford/FilmMagic/Getty Images, p. 67; © Jason Kemplin/Getty Images, p. 68 (bottom); © LAN/CORBIS, p. 69; © Jonathan Alcorn/ ZUMA Press/CORBIS, p. 71; AP Photo/Cash Money/Universal Records, p. 72; © Todd Strand/ Independent Picture Service, p. 73; © Amanda Edwards/Getty Images, p. 74; © Kevin Winter/ AMA2011/Getty Images for AMA, p. 75; © Chad Batka/CORBIS, p. 77; © Kevin Winter/Getty Images, p. 78; AP Photo/FOX/Michael Becker, p. 79; © Walik Goshorn/CORBIS, p. 85; © Jamie McCarthy/WireImages/Getty Images, p. 86; AP Photo/PRNewsFoto/PepsiCo, p. 89; © Dave Kotinsky/Stringer/Getty Images, p. 90; MediaPunch Inc/Rex USA, p. 95.

Front cover: © Danny Martindale/Stringer/Getty Images.
Back cover: © Dan MacMedan/USA TODAY.

Main body text set in USA TODAY Roman Regular 10.5/15.

ABOUT THE AUTHOR

Felicity Britton is a writer and a nonprofit advocate. Originally from Australia, she lives in Minneapolis with her two daughters, Izzy and Luci. She loves parks, travel, movies, and trying new restaurants.